Library of Congress Control Number: 2024951796
ISBN is 979-8-88870-330-4
979-8-88870-379-3 and 979-8-88870-471-4
Copyright 2025 Cathy Garland

All rights reserved. No part of this book may be reproduced, stored in a retrieval system, or transmitted in any form or by any means, electronic, mechanical, photocopying, or otherwise, without the prior written permission of the author.

Among the scriptural translations used or consulted were NLT, MSG, NASB, TPT, and ISV.

Scripture quotations marked NIV are taken from The Holy Bible, New International Version® NIV® Copyright © 1973, 1978, 1984, 2011 by Biblica, Inc. Used with permission.

Scripture quotations marked ISV are taken from the Holy Bible: International Standard Version® Release 2.0. Copyright © 1996-2013 by the ISV Foundation. Used by permission of Davidson Press, LLC. All rights reserved internationally.

Scripture quotations marked NASB are taken from the New American Standard Bible®, Copyright © 1960, 1971, 1977, 1995, 2020 by The Lockman Foundation. Used by permission. All rights reserved.

Scripture quotations marked NLT are taken from the Holy Bible, New Living Translation, Copyright © 1996, 2004, 2015 by Tyndale House Foundation. Used by permission of Tyndale House Publishers, Inc., Carol Stream, Illinois 60188. All rights reserved.

Scripture questions marked MSG are taken from THE MESSAGE: The Bible in Contemporary Language. Copyright © 2002 by Eugene H. Peterson. All rights reserved. THE MESSAGE Numbered Edition Copyright © 2005.

# Special Thanks

A very special thank you to my sister, Tamara, who designed both beautiful covers of my books. Her design talent and artistic eye make my rudimentary ideas blossom.

# Welcome!

When my first husband divorced me, when I lost my first child in miscarriage, when the man I loved (whom I later married) broke up with me for the third time and dated the woman he thought was the woman of his dreams, when I broke my neck in a car accident, when I lost my second child in miscarriage, when I waited ten years for the birth of my son—the list goes on.

It was the revelation of the God who makes and keeps his promises that kept hope alive in me. It was the God who sees me (El Roi) that kept me from losing my faith. It was the God who declares his truth (Jehovah Nissi) about who I am, who I will be at the end of my life, and whose I am, that kept me from believing the lies my circumstances tried to preach. It was knowing—and being known by—God that made all the difference.

As you walk through this devotional, I pray it anchors you to that same truth: that you are deeply loved by God, fully seen, and fully known.

Want a simple way to stay rooted in these truths? Sign up to receive a daily text reminder of that day's name of God. You'll cycle through all the names one by one, and then start again—an ongoing invitation to return to the devotional or simply rest in the truth of who he is, right where you are. Go to revelationship.net/known-signup to receive 31 days of daily text prompts to help you stay focused on who God is and who you are in him.

May you dive deep into the God who knows you better than you know yourself.

*Cathy Colver Garland*

## ABOUT ME

### MOM/AUTHOR/SPEAKER/BIBLE NERD

I'm Cathy Garland, the co-author of the book *Revelationship: Transformative Intimacy With Christ* and *Gracefull Musings*, a blog written for busy moms in that short break before little fingers appear under the bathroom door.

REVELATIONSHIP.NET

# WHO GOD IS → WHO I AM

*Knowing who God is transforms how we see ourselves.*

| God's Identity | What That Means | My Identity In Him |
|---|---|---|
| Abba (Father) | Intimate, loving Father | I am a daughter of the Most High God. (Romans 8:15) |
| Creator | Designer of all things | I am created in his image, knit together in my mother's womb. (Genesis 1:27; Psalm 139:13) |
| El Roi | The God who sees me | I am seen, including what is done to me. (Genesis 16:13) |
| Jehovah Jireh | The Lord who provides | I am cared for and never without his provision. (Genesis 22:14) |
| Jehovah Nissi | The Lord is my banner | I am marked by his truth, not by my past. (Exodus 17:15, Song of Solomon 2:4) |
| Emmanuel | God dwelling with us | I am never alone. (Matthew 1:23) |
| The Potter | He shapes and molds with care | I am hand-crafted for purpose. (Isaiah 64:8) |
| The Good Shepherd | Protector and guide | I am safe, led, and deeply known. (John 10:14) |

# WHO GOD IS → WHO I AM

*Knowing who God is transforms how we see ourselves.*

| God's Identity | What That Means | My Identity In Him |
| --- | --- | --- |
| Resurrection & The Life | He brings life out of death | I am redeemed and eternal life has already begun for me. (John 11:25) |
| Alpha & Omega | Beginning and End | My story is secure in his hands. (Revelation 22:13) |
| Omnipresent | Present in all time and space | He is redeeming my past, with me now, and waiting in my future. (Psalm 139:7–10) |
| El Shaddai | All-sufficient One | Out of his abundance, he is my sufficiency. (Genesis 17:1) |
| Jehovah Rapha | The Lord who heals | I am being healed by his hand, in his timing. (Exodus 15:26) |
| Jehovah Shalom | The Lord our peace | I am held in peace even in trouble. (Judges 6:24) |
| The Vine | Source of life | Connected to him, I flourish. (John 15:5) |
| Jehovah Shammah | The Lord is there | I am never without him. He is here and he is already there. (Ezekiel 48:35) |

# WHO GOD IS → WHO I AM

*Knowing who God is transforms how we see ourselves.*

| God's Identity | What That Means | My Identity In Him |
| --- | --- | --- |
| Jehovah Tzidkenu | The Lord our righteousness | I am clothed in his righteousness. (Jeremiah 23:6) |
| Holy | Perfect, whole, set apart, unchanging | He exchanged his holiness for my sinfulness. Now I am set apart. (1 Peter 1:16; 2 Corinthians 5:21) |
| Faithful & True | Always keeps his word | I can trust him over and over. He is dependable. (Revelation 19:11) |
| Jehovah M'Kaddesh | The Lord who sanctifies | I am being made holy. I reflect his image. (Exodus 31:13) |
| El Olam | Everlasting God | I am part of his eternal story. (Genesis 21:33) |
| Jehovah Qanna | Jealous God | I am deeply valued, pursued for good, not for control. (Exodus 34:14) |
| Jehovah Cherub | The Lord our Sword | I am fought for. The battle is the Lord's. (Psalm 18:10–14) |
| Jehovah Go'el | Kinsman-Redeemer | I am redeemed at great cost. I belong to him. (Isaiah 41:14) |

# WHO GOD IS → WHO I AM

*Knowing who God is transforms how we see ourselves.*

| God's Identity | What That Means | My Identity In Him |
|---|---|---|
| Jehovah Hamelech | The King | I am a citizen of his upside-down Kingdom. (Psalm 47:7) |
| Jehovah Hashopet | The Judge | I am accountable to a just and holy Judge—and justified in Christ. (Judges 11:27) |
| Jehovah Khabodi | My Glory | He is the lifter of my head. I am restored in dignity. (Psalm 3:3) |
| Jehovah Machsi | My Refuge | I am safe and shielded in him. (Psalm 91:2) |
| Jehovah 'Ori | My Light | I am guided, never lost in the dark. (Psalm 27:1) |
| Jehovah Sel'i | My Rock | I am anchored and unshakable in him. (Psalm 18:2) |
| Jehovah Uzzi | My Strength | I am empowered by his might, not my own. (Psalm 28:7) |
| Jehovah Magen | My Shield | I am empowered by his might, not my own. (Psalm 28:7) |

KNOWN DEVOTIONAL | PAGE #7

# ABBA

### VERSES TO CONSIDER:

- Abba, Father, he said, everything is possible for you. Take this cup from me. Yet not what I will, but what you will. — Mark 14:36
- The Spirit you received brought about your adoption to sonship. And by him we cry, "Abba, Father." — Romans 8:15
- Because you are his sons, God sent the Spirit of his Son into our hearts, the Spirit who calls out, "Abba, Father." — Galatians 4:6

### DEVOTIONAL THOUGHT

"Abba" is not the language of formality—it's the language of *belonging*. When Jesus cried out "Abba" in the garden, it was the Son of God appealing to his Father in the most intimate way possible, affirming both God's sovereignty and Jesus' own identity as Son. And here's the miracle: by the Spirit, we get to cry out the same word.

This isn't about sentimentality. It's about access. It's about being welcomed into the deepest intimacy with the Creator of the universe. We're not simply tolerated or observed from a distance. We're invited close. Like the prodigal's father, our Abba runs to meet us. Like a wise and watchful shepherd, he disciplines to protect. This is the Fatherhood of God —not cold formality, but warmth with weight. Majesty wrapped in mercy.

### BECAUSE GOD IS ABBA, I AM...

...secure in my belonging, held by a love that is both intimate and authoritative. I am not abandoned or orphaned—I am claimed, watched over, and welcomed into his arms.

*Abba, Father!*

# ABBA

## JOURNALING PROMPTS

- Where in my life do I relate to God more as a formal judge than an intimate Abba?
- Abba, help me trust in your nearness. Show me how to live like a loved child, not a spiritual orphan.

## PRACTICING HIS PRESENCE

Today, when you feel anxious or uncertain, pause and whisper, "Abba." Let that single word remind you who holds you and whose you are.

Or, take 3 deep breaths, each time breathing in his closeness.
Inhale: "You are my Abba." Exhale: "I am your child."

# ABBA

REFLECT & RESPOND

Today, invite your heart to linger with your Abba through the simple act of writing. Imagine you are sitting at the kitchen table with your Father God, pen in hand, just as you would write a note to an earthly father you love and trust.

Gratefulness Excercise:
Write a letter to Abba, telling him what you are grateful for today. You might:
- Thank him for specific ways he's cared for you.
- Share your joys and concerns.
- Tell him what it means to you to belong to him.

Optional:
If you feel led, turn your letter into a short poem or prayer. Let it be imperfect but heartfelt—your Abba treasures your voice and your words.

# CREATOR

VERSES TO CONSIDER:

- So God created man in his own image… — Genesis 1:27
- For you formed my inward parts; you knitted me together in my mother's womb. — Psalm 139:13

DEVOTIONAL THOUGHT

God didn't just make the mountains and oceans. He made you with precision. With care. With joy. You are not a product of chance or a collection of traits that "just happened." Every part of you—from your fingerprints to your personality—was formed with purpose by the One who called the stars by name.

If you've ever wished you were different, you're not alone. But every time we wish away a piece of ourselves, we risk forgetting who formed us and why. To worship God as Creator is to honor his work even when it's uncomfortable. You were created in his image—not in the image of culture, comparison, or social media trends. And because he created you, he gets to define you. You belong to him. Your life is a canvas that reveals his glory, and he has a plan for every thread he's weaving into your story.

BECAUSE GOD IS CREATOR, I AM…

…not random or accidental. I am his design—woven with intention, purpose, and beauty. I carry his image. I belong to him.

*My Creator*

# CREATOR

## JOURNALING PROMPTS

- Where am I struggling to love or accept part of the way God made me?
- God, show me what you see when you look at me. Remind me I am your design.

..........................................................................................................

..........................................................................................................

..........................................................................................................

..........................................................................................................

..........................................................................................................

..........................................................................................................

..........................................................................................................

..........................................................................................................

## PRACTICING HIS PRESENCE

Take 5 minutes to look at your hands. Really notice them—their strength, shape, scars, fingerprints. Let them remind you: "I am formed by God's hands. I carry his image. I am his.

Or, whenever you catch your reflection today, repeat: "I am fearfully and wonderfully made by a loving Creator.

# CREATOR

REFLECT & RESPOND

Today, pause to consider the beauty of the One who formed you. Just as a painter leaves brushstrokes in a masterpiece, your Creator has left his fingerprints in every part of who you are.

Mindfulness Exercise:
Inside the mirror below, instead of sketching your reflection, write words that reflect the truth of who God made you to be. You might include:
- Traits of your character that reflect God's nature (kindness, creativity, perseverance)
- Talents or skills he has entrusted to you
- Physical features or personal quirks you genuinely like about yourself
- Spiritual gifts or passions that bring you joy

When you've finished, take a moment to thank him for each word you've written. This is his handiwork—crafted with care, treasured beyond measure.

# EL ROI

### VERSES TO CONSIDER:

- She gave this name to the Lord who spoke to her: "You are the God who sees me,' for she said, 'I have now seen the One who sees me." — Genesis 16:13
- And even the very hairs of your head are all numbered. — Matthew 10:30
- For the eyes of the Lord are on the righteous, and his ears are open to their prayer. But the face of the Lord is against those who do evil. — 1 Peter 3:12

### DEVOTIONAL THOUGHT

Hagar wasn't powerful or favored. She was a slave. A woman. An outsider. She didn't get to choose her circumstances, and when it all became too much, she ran into the wilderness. Into isolation. But not beyond the eyes of God.

It was there, in the desert, that God met her with tenderness and a promise. And in that moment, she gave him a name no one had ever spoken before: El Roi, which means the God who sees me.

Maybe today you feel unseen. Misunderstood. Pushed to the sidelines or crushed under the weight of someone else's decisions. But God sees you—not from a distance, but up close. Not just your circumstances, but your heart. He sees the betrayal, the exhaustion, the tears behind the smile. And just like he did for Hagar, he draws near.

### BECAUSE GOD IS EL ROI, I AM...

...never invisible. I am seen by the One who knows the full story, including what's been done to me, what I've carried, what I've hidden, and what I've hoped. I am not overlooked. I am known.

*El Roi*

# EL ROI

## JOURNALING PROMPTS

- Where in my life do I feel unseen or misunderstood?
- God, show me how you're meeting me in the places I feel invisible. Help me see your eyes on me.

............................................................................................................................................

............................................................................................................................................

............................................................................................................................................

............................................................................................................................................

............................................................................................................................................

............................................................................................................................................

............................................................................................................................................

............................................................................................................................................

## PRACTICING HIS PRESENCE

Throughout the day, pause and repeat this truth: "You are the God who sees me. I am not alone."

Or, write down one moment today when you felt unacknowledged, unsupported, or unnoticed. Take a moment to let it sink in that God noticed. Let that knowledge remind you: El Roi is near, even in the wilderness.

# EL ROI

REFLECT & RESPOND

Today, pause to consider the beauty of the One who formed you. Just as a painter leaves brushstrokes in a masterpiece, your Creator has left his fingerprints in every part of who you are.

Mindfulness Exercise:
Take a quiet walk today somewhere familiar, if you can. As you walk, ask God to help you see with his eyes. Notice the small things you might have overlooked before: the lacework on the back of a leaf, the sound of birds in the distance, the way sunlight filters through branches, or the pattern of cracks on the sidewalk.

Let each detail remind you that El Roi—the God who sees—misses nothing. He notices beauty in the ordinary, and he notices you. When you return, write down what caught your attention and thank him for the gift of being fully seen and known.

# JEHOVAH JIREH

VERSES TO CONSIDER:

- So Abraham called the name of that place, "The Lord will provide"; as it is said to this day, "On the mount of the Lord it shall be provided." — Genesis 22:14
- And my God will meet all your needs according to the riches of his glory in Christ Jesus. — Philippians 4:19

DEVOTIONAL THOUGHT

Jehovah Jireh means "God who provides." Provision means "to see beforehand." That's what God does. He sees the need before it even exists and makes a way.

Abraham experienced this on the mountain. As he raised the knife in obedience, God provided a ram. A substitute. A rescue. A picture of the ultimate provision to come: Jesus. The provision didn't come before the test—it came in the middle of obedience. Jehovah Jireh wasn't just willing to provide. He did so right on time.

Perhaps the answer to your need hasn't appeared yet. The pressure's real, but he isn't scrambling. What you need is already seen, already in motion.

His provision isn't just stuff. It's often peace, strength, and daily bread. And it never depends on your ability, but on his nature. And he has never failed to come through.

BECAUSE GOD IS JEHOVAH JIREH, I AM…

…cared for. I am not forgotten, abandoned, or overlooked. I am never without his provision. My life is in the hands of a God who sees ahead and supplies what I need in his perfect timing.

*Jehovah Jireh*

# JEHOVAH JIREH

## JOURNALING PROMPTS

- Where do I need to trust God as my provider?
- Lord, help me release control and step forward in obedience, even before I see how you'll provide.

.................................................................................................................

.................................................................................................................

.................................................................................................................

.................................................................................................................

.................................................................................................................

.................................................................................................................

.................................................................................................................

.................................................................................................................

## PRACTICING HIS PRESENCE

As you go through your day, watch for small ways God is caring for you—a kind word, an unexpected gift, a burst of energy, a moment of clarity. Name each one: "This is your provision too."

Or, take one need that feels heavy today. Write it down and physically hand the paper to God in prayer. Say: "Jehovah Jireh, this is yours now."

# JEHOVAH JIREH

REFLECT & RESPOND

Today, focus on the God who provides for you—sometimes in ways large and visible, and often in quiet, unexpected moments.

Prompt:
Create a Gratitude Jar to celebrate God's provision in your life. You can use the template provided on the next page to color your own jar, or use a real jar at home.
- Each time you notice a way God has provided—whether it's a kind word, a small gift, a moment of clarity, or a burst of energy. Write it on a slip of paper (or a heart cutout) and place it in the jar.
- Label it with the date or a brief note if you like.
- Over time, watch your jar fill up, reminding you that Jehovah Jireh is faithful to meet your needs.

Optional Reflection:
Take a few minutes at the end of the week to read through the slips in your jar. Name each one aloud, saying:
"Jehovah Jireh, this is your provision."

Let your heart be filled with gratitude as you celebrate God's faithfulness in the small and large ways of daily life.

# JEHOVAH NISSI

VERSES TO CONSIDER:

- And Moses built an altar and called the name of it, The Lord is my banner. — Exodus 17:15
- He brought me to the banqueting house, and his banner over me was love. — Song of Solomon 2:4

DEVOTIONAL THOUGHT

In battle, armies raised banners to mark identity, claim territory, and rally strength. On the field against Amalek, Moses lifted his hands to obey God, and God gave victory. Afterward, Moses named that place Jehovah Nissi because he recognized the true source of their strength was the Lord.

God still goes before us today. His banner over us declares who we belong to—not our sin, not our past, not the voice of the accuser. His banner is love. It reminds us that we're redeemed, not ruined. He calls us his own.

When the battle feels relentless and your story feels marked by failure, lift your eyes to the banner of truth. His love is the sign over your life. His name is your covering.

BECAUSE GOD IS JEHOVAH NISSI, I AM...

...marked by his truth, not by my past. I don't carry the labels of shame, failure, or fear. I live under his banner of victory and love.

*Jehovah Nissi*

# JEHOVAH NISSI

## JOURNALING PROMPTS

- Where have I been letting my past or pain define me more than God's truth?
- What would it look like to stand under his banner today?

## PRACTICING HIS PRESENCE

When you feel overwhelmed, pause and imagine his banner waving over you. Whisper, "You are Jehovah Nissi, and I am covered by your love."

Or, when something from your past reminds you of failure or mistakes made, surrender them to the one whose banner declares his unconditional love for you.

# JEHOVAH NISSI

REFLECT & RESPOND

Today, dwell on the truth that God's banner of love and victory waves over you—covering, protecting, and claiming you as his own.

Prompt:
Create a personal Jehovah Nissi banner exercise:
1. Take a piece of paper and draw a small banner, flag, or even just a rectangle.
2. Inside the banner, write:
   - Words or phrases that represent struggles, fears, or past mistakes you want to surrender to God
   - Scriptures or affirmations that remind you of God's victory and protection
3. As you write, visualize God holding this banner over you. Imagine his love and protection spreading out, covering every worry, fear, or regret.

Optional Creative Expansion:
- Color or decorate your banner as a visual reminder of God's protection.
- Keep it somewhere you'll see it daily (a mirror, desk, or journal page) to remind you that you are covered by his love and victory.

# EMMANUEL

## VERSES TO CONSIDER:

- Behold, the virgin shall conceive and bear a son, and they shall call his name Emmanuel (which means, God with us). — Matthew 1:23
- Where shall I go from your Spirit? Or where shall I flee from your presence? — Psalm 139:7

## DEVOTIONAL THOUGHT

God never wanted distance. From the beginning, his desire was to dwell with us. Emmanuel means "God with us"—not occasionally, not conditionally, but dwelling with us forever. Jesus came not just to rescue us from sin and death, but to restore what was lost in Eden: presence. Relationship. Nearness.

When Jesus died, the temple curtain tore in two from top to bottom. The separation between God and man was removed forever. Now, through his Spirit, he lives within us. We never have to fight for God's attention or earn our way into his presence. He is with us in every ordinary moment and every aching one.

Even when the world feels loud or life feels lonely, Emmanuel has not left. He walks with us. He holds us. And he speaks, not from a distance or a mountain, but from within.

## BECAUSE GOD IS EMMANUEL, I AM…

…never alone. His presence surrounds me—before me, behind me, within me. I don't have to strive to find him. He is already here.

# EMMANUEL

## JOURNALING PROMPTS

- Where have I felt alone or distant lately?
- How might I become more aware of God's nearness in this space?

................................................................................

................................................................................

................................................................................

................................................................................

................................................................................

................................................................................

................................................................................

................................................................................

## PRACTICING HIS PRESENCE

Take five quiet minutes today. Breathe deeply. Whisper, "You are here." Then wait in silence, trusting his presence to meet you.

Or, open the Bible and surrender your time with him. Trust that his presence will come and guide you.

# EMMANUEL

REFLECT & RESPOND (PERSONAL)

Today, dwell on the truth that God is not far away. He is Emmanuel—always near, always with us. His presence isn't something we earn or chase; it is a gift that surrounds us in every moment.

Prompt: Create an Emmanuel empty chair exercise
- Find a quiet spot and place an empty chair beside you.
- Imagine Jesus sitting in that chair—present, attentive, full of love.
- Speak to him as you would a close friend. Share your fears, joys, or even the ordinary details of your day.
- Then pause. Sit together in silence. Rest in the truth that he is with you, listening and holding you in his presence.

Optional Creative Expansion
- Write a short note or prayer as if you were handing it to Jesus in the chair.
- Leave the chair in view for the day as a visual reminder: you are never alone.
- Return to it whenever you need to remember his nearness.

# EMMANUEL

REFLECT & RESPOND (FOR OTHERS)

Next, consider how God's presence flows through you to others. Emmanuel means God is with us, and that presence can be tangible in the way we show love and care. Whether we sow a small seed of kindness or accomplish something "big" when we do it out of the overflow of God's life-giving presence, we can trust the results or the "fruit" to him.

Prompt:
- Think of one person in your life who could experience God's presence through your actions today. Write a short note, make a small gift, or do a simple act that sows seeds of kindness.
- Or, ask God at the beginning of your day to arrange an appointment for you to show God's presence by being God's hands and feet to someone today.
- As you act, silently say: "Emmanuel, may your presence be shown through me."

Optional Creative Expansion:
- Reflect on the nativity story: imagine being part of the first Christmas scene, seeing God come near in a baby.
- Write a short prayer connecting the miracle of God coming near then to the ways you can reflect his presence now.
- Create a small visual reminder (a drawing, a symbol, or a sticker) that represents you being hands and feet for God today.

# THE POTTER

VERSES TO CONSIDER:

- But now, O Lord, you are our Father; we are the clay, and you are our potter; we are all the work of your hand. — Isaiah 64:8
- So I went down to the potter's house, and there he was working at his wheel... But the pot he was shaping... was marred... so the potter formed it into another pot, shaping it as seemed best to him. — Jeremiah 18:3-4

DEVOTIONAL THOUGHT

You are not random. You are not ruined. You are clay in the hands of a perfect Potter who sees the end from the beginning. He spins the wheel of your life with intention, applying just enough pressure to form you, not break you. When something mars the design, he does not discard the clay. He begins again, shaping you into something beautiful and useful.

The Potter doesn't just make you *into* something; he shapes you *for* something. Every circumstance, every stretch of pressure, every quiet season when you feel forgotten is all part of the shaping. He holds the vision. He sees what you cannot. Even when you feel unfinished, you are in process, in purpose, in his hands.

As I've studied the holiness and goodness of God, I've found myself captivated by the name Israel. While most of our Bibles define the name as "one who wrestles with God," that's only scratching the surface. A group of scholars (see footnotes) suggests a far more layered meaning: "He retains God," or more fully, "He has become a vessel in which God can be received and retained."

*A vessel in which God can be received and retained.*

This is what the Potter is shaping us into: not just something useful, but someone holy enough, humble enough, whole enough to receive and retain his presence. It's what Jacob "won" when he wrestled with God. Not merely a name, not just a blessing, but a new identity fit for God's indwelling.

# THE POTTER

## DEVOTIONAL THOUGHT (CONTINUED)

Look at Jacob's journey: deception, disconnection, disillusionment. All of his striving, all of his controlling—it led him to a night of surrender. He thought he'd face Esau, but instead, he faced God. He came away limping, renamed, and forever marked.

While Jacob had always chased the inheritance, God had always pursued the indwelling. "I will be your God, and you will be mine, and I will dwell with you." That's the real prize: God's presence.

Since Eden, God has been seeking vessels that would contain and pour out his presence. By grace, we are being formed into vessels of the same kind.

You may feel ordinary, marred, or in process, but in the Potter's hands, you are being shaped to carry the presence of the Holy. Not just once, but always.

## BECAUSE GOD IS THE POTTER, I AM...

...hand-crafted for purpose. I am not mass-produced or accidental. I am the work of his hands, formed with vision and care.

*The Potter*

# THE POTTER

## JOURNALING PROMPTS

- Where do I resist being shaped into a vessel that receives God's presence?
- Where am I striving for blessing more than intimacy?

## PRACTICING HIS PRESENCE

When you feel pressure—emotional, circumstantial, spiritual—say aloud: "Shape me to receive You here, Potter. Make me a vessel that retains You."

Let surrender replace striving. Let your identity be found not in what you do, but in Whom you are held.

# THE POTTER

REFLECT & RESPOND

Today, reflect on the truth that God is shaping you with intention, like clay in a master's hands. Your identity is found in him, not in your performance.

Prompt:
- Take a small piece of clay, playdough, or even silly putty. As you shape it with your hands, consider how God is shaping your life:
  - What areas of your heart or mind need molding?
  - What habits or attitudes might he be gently reshaping?
- While molding, repeat silently or aloud: "Potter, shape me to receive your image. Make me a vessel through which your Spirit can flow."

Optional Journaling Expansion:
- After the physical exercise, journal about what came to mind while shaping the clay:
  - Were there places you resisted the shaping?
  - How does it feel to let God mold you instead of trying to control or fix yourself?
  - Write a short prayer of surrender for the areas of your life you want him to continue shaping.

WE ARE THE CLAY, AND YOU ARE OUR POTTER; WE ARE ALL THE WORK OF YOUR HAND. – ISAIAH 64:8

# THE GOOD SHEPHERD

**VERSES TO CONSIDER:**

- I am the good shepherd; I know my sheep and my sheep know me." — John 10:14
- He tends his flock like a shepherd: He gathers the lambs in his arms and carries them close to his heart. — Isaiah 40:11

**DEVOTIONAL THOUGHT**

There's something so tender about how Scripture speaks of shepherds. Jesus isn't just a competent leader or a watchful protector—he calls himself the Good Shepherd. Good, as in faithful. Good, as in gentle. Good, as in willing to lay down his life for the sheep.

Some sheep are strong, fast, and confident. But others are rejected by their mothers, cast off, and unlikely to survive without special care. These are called "bummer lambs." A shepherd knows what to do so that he does not lose the lamb to lack of care. He carries that lamb close, feeds it by hand, lets it sleep on his chest so it hears his heartbeat. And when it grows strong enough to return to the flock, that lamb never forgets who saved it. Because of this care, this sheep knows the shepherd's voice better than the others.

Maybe you feel like a bummer lamb—rejected, forgotten, weak. But to the Good Shepherd, you are not a burden. You're beloved by Jehovah Raah, the Lord Our Shepherd. He carries you close until you're steady again. And in the process, you come to know his voice in a way others might not. You were never left out. You were drawn in.

**BECAUSE GOD IS THE GOOD SHEPHERD, I AM...**

...safe, seen, and led. I am not rejected—I am deeply known and tenderly carried. I can recognize his voice when he calls to me.

*The Good Shepherd*

# THE GOOD SHEPHERD

## JOURNALING PROMPTS

- Where have I felt forgotten, unseen, or unworthy—and how might the Good Shepherd be drawing me closer in that very place?

........................................................................................................

........................................................................................................

........................................................................................................

........................................................................................................

........................................................................................................

........................................................................................................

........................................................................................................

........................................................................................................

## PRACTICING HIS PRESENCE

Today, when you feel stressed or unseen, pause and whisper: "You are my Shepherd. I am known and carried."

Imagine being that bummer lamb, rejected by another, but resting on the Shepherd's chest, hearing his voice. What does he say to you?

# THE GOOD SHEPHERD

REFLECT & RESPOND

Today, reflect on the tender care of your Shepherd, who knows you by name and carries you through every season.

Prompt:
- Take a quiet moment and imagine a peaceful pasture or hillside. Visualize yourself as one of the sheep in the Shepherd's care.
- Ask yourself:
  - How does it feel to be fully known and cared for?
  - What burdens could I lay down into his hands today?
- In your journal, write a letter or short prayer to the Shepherd:
  - Describe what you are grateful for in his care.
  - Share what you need him to carry for you right now.
  - Record the "voice" of the Shepherd—what encouragement, guidance, or reassurance comes to your heart in this exercise.

# I AM THE GOOD Shepherd

I KNOW MY SHEEP AND MY SHEEP KNOW ME.—JOHN 10:14

# RESURRECTION & LIFE

**VERSES TO CONSIDER:**

- I am the resurrection and the life. The one who believes in me will live, even though they die. — John 11:25
- And you, who were dead in your trespasses...God made alive together with him. — Colossians 2:13

**DEVOTIONAL THOUGHT**

So if Jesus is the resurrection and the life, what does that make us? Quite simply: without him, we are dead. Not just tired or off track, but spiritually lifeless. The resurrection of Lazarus wasn't just a miracle; it was also a shadow of what was to come. Jesus was showing us what he came to do—not just raise the dead, but bring life to those who are walking around spiritually empty.

Paul said it plainly: "You were dead... but God made you alive together with him" (Colossians 2:13). This isn't future-tense resurrection. This is now. Eternal life doesn't begin after death, as some believe. Eternal life begins the moment we believe. We are no longer in bondage. No longer powerless. We are people of the resurrection, alive with the very Spirit who raised Christ from the grave.

But it doesn't stop there. We are not only made alive, we are sent to *spread* life. We carry resurrection hope into dying places. The same Jesus who called Lazarus out of the tomb calls us into a life of purpose: to continue his ministry of making all things new.

**BECAUSE GOD IS THE RESURRECTION & LIFE, I AM...**

...not defined by death—spiritual or physical. I am redeemed, alive in Christ, and already walking in eternal life.

*Resurrection & Life*

# RESURRECTION & LIFE

## JOURNALING PROMPTS

- Where in my life am I still living as if I'm spiritually dead or powerless?
- What would it look like to live fully alive in Christ today?

## PRACTICING HIS PRESENCE

When you feel stuck in old patterns, pause and whisper: "I am alive in Christ. This is not who I am anymore."

Or, on your walk or drive today, ask God to show you one person or situation where he's inviting you to speak life and hope, just as Jesus did at Lazarus' tomb.

# RESURRECTION & LIFE

REFLECT & RESPOND

Today, dwell on the truth that you are not powerless, not stuck, not defined by your past. Jesus is the resurrection and the life. And because he lives in you, you are fully alive. The same Spirit that raised Christ from the grave now breathes new life into your identity, your story, and your future.

Prompt: Speak Life Over Yourself (Identity Statements)
- Take a piece of paper and write down the lies or "deadening words" you've believed about yourself (e.g., I'll never change, I'm not enough, I'm stuck).
- Cross them out boldly as a visual act of surrender.
- Beneath each one, write a resurrection truth rooted in Scripture (e.g., I am alive in Christ, I am chosen, I am free, I am made new).
- Speak these truths aloud as declarations over your life, letting your own voice remind you who you really are in him.

Examples of "I AM" Scriptural Declarations
- I am a new creation (2 Corinthians 5:17)
- I am alive with Christ (Colossians 2:13)
- I am God's workmanship (Ephesians 2:10)
- I am chosen and dearly loved (Colossians 3:12)
- I am free in Christ (Galatians 5:1)
- I am never alone (Matthew 28:20)

For a deep dive into Biblical declarations vs. worldly affirmations visit:
https://cathy544.wixsite.com/gracefullgarlands/spiritual-declarations

HE IS NOT HERE,

*He is risen...*

MATTHEW 28:6

# ALPHA & OMEGA

### VERSES TO CONSIDER:

- I am the Alpha and the Omega, says the Lord God, who is, and who was, and who is to come, the Almighty. — Revelation 1:8
- Jesus Christ is the same yesterday and today and forever. — Hebrews 13:8

### DEVOTIONAL THOUGHT

We tend to live in the middle of things, between the what-was and the not-yet. In that in-between, we can lose sight of where we're going, or forget that God was ever in our beginning. But Jesus isn't just a part of our story; he is the story's Author and its Finisher. He declares himself the Alpha and the Omega, which are the first and last letters of the Greek alphabet. Saying this was a way of saying, "I hold it all."

He was there before you breathed your first. He is present in the questions, the mess, and the waiting. And he not only knows how this ends—with redemption, restoration, and glory—*but in his omnipresence, he is already there!* Even when life feels out of sequence, he is steady, sovereign, and never in a hurry.

When we root our identity in his timeline instead of our own, we can live with courage. Our lives are chapters in a divine narrative he is still writing, not random episodes. Knowing this gives us permission and strength to trust the process.

### BECAUSE GOD IS THE ALPHA & OMEGA, I AM...

...never outside of his timing, my story is not defined by one chapter, and I am already fully, eternally, and lovingly known.

*Alpha & Omega*

# ALPHA & OMEGA

## JOURNALING PROMPTS

- Where am I tempted to believe that God has forgotten me or that my story is off track?
- What would it look like to trust him with the middle, knowing he's already written the end?

_____
_____
_____
_____
_____
_____
_____

## PRACTICING HIS PRESENCE

As you go through your day, whisper this truth over your heart:
"You were in my beginning. You hold my now. You've already seen the end."

Let that shape how you respond to stress, uncertainty, or delay.

# ALPHA & OMEGA

REFLECT & RESPOND

God knows how easily we forget. That's why, after Israel crossed the Jordan on dry ground, He instructed them to set up stones of remembrance. Each stone was a testimony to God's power, provision, and presence. These stones were for the generations to come, physical markers that declared, "Here is where God showed up."

In the same way, we need tangible reminders of God's faithfulness in our lives. Moments when He carried us, delivered us, or spoke to us. When doubts creep in or struggles overwhelm us, these markers become steady witnesses pointing back to His unchanging goodness.

Building Stone Markers of Remembrance
1. Gather Your Stones
2. Find several smooth, flat stones small enough to hold in your hand, but large enough to write on. If possible, choose stones that can stack on top of each other.
3. Mark Each Stone
4. On each stone, write a word, phrase, or short verse that represents a moment when God was faithful to you. (Examples: Provision, Healing, Forgiveness, Psalm 23:1)
5. Stack Them Up
6. Carefully stack your stones somewhere visible—in your home, garden, or Prayer Corner. As you see them, let them remind you of the foundation of God's work in your life.
1. Tell the Story
2. Each time someone notices your "stone markers," share the story of what God did. Just like Israel, your testimony can strengthen faith in others.
1. Pray Over Your Stones
2. Pray aloud: "God, thank You for these markers of Your faithfulness. May they remind me—and others—of who You are, what You've done, and the hope I have in You."

"I AM the ALPHA and the OMEGA the FIRST and the LAST the BEGINNING AND the END."

# OMNIPRESENT

VERSES TO CONSIDER:

- "Where shall I go from your Spirit? Or where shall I flee from your presence? If I ascend to heaven, you are there! If I make my bed in Sheol, you are there!
  — Psalm 139:7–8 (ESV)

DEVOTIONAL THOUGHT

God's omnipresence can be a transformational revelation.

He is not simply everywhere in space; he is fully present in all of time. Past, present, and future are laid before him not as unfolding moments to anticipate or that he "foreknows," but as a reality he already occupies. He is *there*. Right now, he is still laying the foundations of the earth (Job 38:4). He is still knitting us together in the womb (Psalm 139:13). He is with us in this present moment (Hebrews 13:5), and he is already in the future, victorious and unshaken (Isaiah 52:12).

We are bound to time. We move through it one breath, one decision, one experience at a time. But God is not like us. He exists outside of the boundaries of time, unchanging, eternal. And yet he fills our time completely. He walks with us and reveals himself in ways we can know and experience. *These revelations transform us.*

The Bible's revelations of God demand a response. His words are not abstract. His words are living, personal, and powerful. They are emanations of his very nature. He speaks, and oceans teem with life. He breathes, and humanity rises from the dust. When we see that God's omnipresence is inseparable from his immutability, holiness, and perfection, we realize something staggering: God is not merely present *with* us—he is present *for* us.

# OMNIPRESENT

### DEVOTIONAL THOUGHT (CONTINUED)

Because he is eternal and unchanging, we can trust that his promises are not bound to a timeline or context. They are still alive—active across all time because they were spoken by a God who fully inhabits all of time, at the same time. And these promises are meant for us because they are directly related to his unchangeable character. He fulfills his Word because of who he is: not just a God of the past, or a hope for the future, but a living, holy, ever-present God who is.

This changes how we see everything:
– Our present circumstances are seen through his unshakable presence
– Our fears of the past are quelled by the God who is present in the past, redeeming it
– Our future (and our fears about it) belongs to God, who is already victorious in it
– Our suffering is reframed by his eternal compassion
– Our worship shifts from obligation to awe
– Our view of our own stories is no longer limited by the present moment because we are caught up in a divine, eternal reality already written in his heart.

### BECAUSE GOD IS OMNIPRESENT, I AM...

...free to live without fear of the past, present, or the future because they belong to the God who is present in all of them, all at the same time.

# OMNIPRESENT

## JOURNALING PROMPTS

- Where am I living as if I'm alone, carrying things God has already offered to carry with me?
- What might change if I truly believed he is already present in my past, fully with me now, and already victorious in my future?

## PRACTICING HIS PRESENCE

When you feel overwhelmed by time—rushed by the present, haunted by the past, or afraid of the future—pause and pray: "You are here. You are still there. You always will be. Time doesn't limit you, and I am held by you outside of it."

Let this truth slow your pace, soften your striving, and settle your spirit. Return to it when you're tempted to control what only God sees fully.

# OMNIPRESENT

REFLECT & RESPOND

Today, dwell on the truth that God is not limited by time. He is not just here in the present moment, but he was there in your past, he is with you now, and he is already in your future. His presence isn't bound by clocks, deadlines, or circumstances. Because He fully inhabits all of time, you are held by him across every moment of your life.

Prompt: Daily Time Journal – Noticing God Across Time
1. Set aside 5–10 quiet minutes at the end of your day.
2. Take a piece of paper, notebook, or journal, and create three columns:
    - Gratitude – Write the things you are thankful for today.
    - God's Voice/Teaching – Note moments where you sensed his presence, guidance, or comfort.
    - Looking Forward – Record what you anticipate, hope for, or are entrusting to him tomorrow.
3. As you write, reflect on how God has been present in your past, is walking with you in the present, and is already faithful in the future.

Optional Creative Expansion
- Use colors, symbols, or doodles to visually mark each column—maybe a sunrise for gratitude, a heart for God's teaching, and a star for hope in tomorrow.
- Keep your journal where you can see it daily as a reminder that God is omnipresent and unchanging.
- At the start of the next day, read the previous entry and whisper: "You were there. You are here. You will always be there."

Example Reflections
- Gratitude: Thankful for a kind conversation with a friend today.
- God's Voice/Teaching: I sensed God's patience with me during a stressful moment at work.
- Looking Forward: Praying for clarity and courage in a meeting tomorrow.

# EL SHADDAI

VERSES TO CONSIDER:

- When Abram was ninety-nine years old, the Lord appeared to him and said, "I am El Shaddai—God Almighty. Serve me faithfully and live a blameless life." — Genesis 17:1
- And may you have the power to understand…how wide, how long, how high, and how deep his love is. — Ephesians 3:18

DEVOTIONAL THOUGHT

El Shaddai is more than a name. To the Hebrew hearer, it was a declaration of God's nature toward his people. Not merely a title of strength, but a declaration of sufficiency that echoes through covenant, wilderness, manger, and cross. In a world ruled by scarcity and striving, this name slices through our anxiety with a truth that stills the soul: He is not the God of just enough. He is the God of *more than enough*.

We often speak of Jesus as "God with us," and rightly so. The miracle of the Incarnation stirs our hearts. We marvel that he walked among us, bore our griefs, felt the cold of night and the sting of betrayal. We relate to his humanity, and in that familiarity, we are comforted. But we must also lift our eyes and remember: the infant wrapped in cloth is no ordinary child. He is El Shaddai: the God who first thundered his name to Abraham beneath a canopy of stars, the God of covenant and cosmos. The Promiser of promises is also the promise fulfilled.

The name El Shaddai is richly layered. Scholars trace it to ideas of mountain-like strength, motherly sustenance, and divine sufficiency. But at its core, it tells us this: "Out of My abundance, I am your sufficiency." Not a rationed provision or an emergency backup, but a steady, overflowing source of life, protection, and covenant love. When God introduces himself as El Shaddai, he isn't merely flexing his power—he's committing his heart.

# EL SHADDAI

## DEVOTIONAL THOUGHT (CONTINUED)

That same sufficiency lies in the manger. We celebrate the birth of Christ not only because he understands our weakness, but because he is the answer to it. There's nothing half-measured or reluctant about his coming. He binds himself to us with full intention, knowing the cost, then pays it in full.

Wrapped in humanity, he is the all-sufficient God who would not be distant. The Creator who feeds the sparrows became the Bread of Life, broken to feed us. The One who shelters and defends his people became the Lamb, slain to cover us.

El Shaddai fills every hollow place we carry. Our emotional hunger, our spiritual thirst, our weariness, our fear—none of it surprises him. He doesn't scold our need; he meets it. Every gap is grace-filled in him. This is the way he designed it.

This, then, is the miracle of Advent: our abundant sufficiency has come. And his name is Jesus.

## BECAUSE GOD IS EL SHADDAI, I AM…

…not "barely sustained," I am filled by his fullness. I am nourished, protected, and kept by the abundance of his love.

# EL SHADDAI

## JOURNALING PROMPTS

- Where have I been living as though God is just barely enough or not enough at all?
- What would it look like to truly trust El Shaddai's sufficiency in that place?

## PRACTICING HIS PRESENCE

Today, when you feel overwhelmed or under-resourced, place your hand over your heart and breathe deeply. Whisper:
"El Shaddai, you are more than enough for me."

Let this become the rhythm of your rest.

# EL SHADDAI

REFLECT & RESPOND

Today, dwell on the truth that God is not a God of scarcity. He is El Shaddai—the God whose provision is mountain-high, river-deep, and overflowing beyond measure. Whatever you lack, whatever feels insufficient, His sufficiency meets you there. You are not holding out for "just enough"; you are resting in the steady abundance of a God who is more than enough.

Prompt: Visual Overflow Exercise
1. Take a piece of paper and a pen or colored pencils.
2. Draw a simple image to represent God's provision. This could be a mountain, a river, a cup, or any symbol that reflects abundance to you.
3. Around your image, write or doodle the areas of your life where you feel need, scarcity, or pressure (for example: finances, relationships, energy, peace, courage).
4. As you focus on each area, visualize God's overflowing supply filling it abundantly. Imagine his love, provision, and strength pouring in until the area feels full, overflowing, and satisfied.
5. Whisper a simple prayer with each area: "El Shaddai, you are more than enough here."

# JEHOVAH RAPHA

### VERSES TO CONSIDER:

- I am the Lord, who heals you. — Exodus 15:26
- By faith in His name, His name itself has made this man strong...perfect health in the presence of all of you. — Acts 3:16 (NRSV)

### DEVOTIONAL THOUGHT

In Exodus, God reveals himself to his people not as a distant observer of suffering but as Yahweh Rapha, the Lord who heals. Not "might heal," or "has healed in the past," but who heals. Healing is not just what he does; it's who he is.

We often long for healing in the visible places: bodies, relationships, finances. And sometimes, by his mercy, we see immediate, miraculous change, such as the man at the temple gate who leapt to his feet when Peter spoke the name of Jesus (Acts 3). But deeper still, beneath every physical restoration, is the soul-healing work only God can do. That is the miracle that lasts.

This is the heart of Yahweh Rapha: not just to make us functional, but whole. He doesn't hand us bandages and send us on our way. He steps into our brokenness, names it, holds it, and restores us from the root. Sometimes the healing is swift, and sometimes it's slow, but it's always sacred.

### BECAUSE GOD IS JEHOVAH RAPHA, I AM...

...not stuck in what's broken. I am not forgotten in my weakness. I am seen, known, and being made whole—from the inside out.

*Jehovah Rapha*

# JEHOVAH RAPHA

## JOURNALING PROMPTS

- Where in my life am I longing for healing?
- What might God want to restore in me that runs deeper than the surface?

................................................................................

................................................................................

................................................................................

................................................................................

................................................................................

................................................................................

................................................................................

## PRACTICING HIS PRESENCE

Today, when you notice pain—physical or emotional—pause and say: "Yahweh Rapha, you are healing me even here. I trust your process."

Or, take a short walk and notice signs of restoration in creation—buds returning to trees, wounds healing over, animals fed. Let these visible signs remind you: healing is already underway.

# JEHOVAH RAPHA

REFLECT & RESPOND

Throughout Scripture, oil is a symbol of God's Spirit—his consecrating, healing presence set apart for his people (see James 5:14, Psalm 23:5, Isaiah 61:1). Anointing with oil is not about the oil itself, but about remembering that the Lord who heals has marked you as his own, and he is present to restore what is broken.

Healing Anointing Exercise
- Take a small amount of olive oil (or any oil you have on hand).
- Read James 5:14 aloud: "Is anyone among you sick? Let them call the elders of the church to pray over them and anoint them with oil in the name of the Lord."
- Gently place a dab of oil on areas that need healing—your heart (emotions), your mind (thoughts), your ears (what you listen to), or any place of physical pain.
- As you anoint each spot, pray simply: "Yahweh Rapha, You are my healer here."
- Rest for a few quiet moments, allowing his Spirit to minister to you.

# JEHOVAH SHALOM

VERSES TO CONSIDER:

- Then Gideon built an altar there to the Lord and called it, "The Lord is Peace." — Judges 6:24 (ESV)
- You keep him in perfect peace whose mind is stayed on you, because he trusts in you. — Isaiah 26:3 (ESV)

DEVOTIONAL THOUGHT

Gideon was threshing wheat in hiding when God revealed himself as Jehovah Shalom. The Midianite oppression had crushed Israel's spirit, and Gideon's questions were raw: "If the Lord is with us, why then has all this happened?" (Judges 6:13). It's here, in the tension of doubt and fear, that God speaks—not with rebuke, but reassurance: "Peace to you. Do not fear; you shall not die." (Judges 6:23). In response, Gideon builds an altar and declares what had just been revealed to his soul: "The Lord is Peace."

Jehovah Shalom does not wait for our understanding to be clear or our hearts to be strong. He meets us in our lowest, most hidden places and reminds us that peace is not found in changed circumstances but in his unchanging presence. His peace quiets the fear that asks if he has abandoned us. His presence silences the lie that we are alone. He is our peace: stronger than our fear, closer than our heartbeat, and faithful to remain.

BECAUSE GOD IS JEHOVAH SHALOM, I AM…

…confidently peaceful. I don't have to wait for my circumstances to change to be still. I can rest in the middle of the storm. I am not alone. I am held by the One who is peace itself.

*Jehovah Shalom*

# JEHOVAH SHALOM

JOURNALING PROMPTS

- Where do I feel most anxious or unsettled right now? What would it look like to meet Jehovah Shalom there?
- God, what am I believing about You that's fueling my fear? Help me see you as you really are—my peace.

PRACTICING HIS PRESENCE

When fear and anxiety creep in today, whisper this truth aloud: "Jehovah Shalom, you are with me. You are my peace."

Or, pause in a quiet place. Breathe slowly and thank God for one area or time where his peace held you, even when things didn't make sense.

# JEHOVAH SHALOM

REFLECT & RESPOND

God's peace is not a distant idea; it is a presence that meets us in our unrest. Surrendering our fears and anxieties allows hi to fill those spaces with his perfect calm (see Judges 6:23, Isaiah 26:3). Practicing intentional release reminds us that peace is found in him, not in changing circumstances.

Surrender and Receive Exercise
1. Sit in a quiet place and rest your hands palms down on your lap.
2. Bring to mind situations, worries, or fears that weigh on you. In prayer, release each one, imagining it falling from your palms. Whisper: "Jehovah Shalom, I surrender this to You."
3. Slowly turn your palms upward, inviting God's peace to fill you. Whisper: "Jehovah Shalom, You are my peace here."
4. Rest in his presence for a few moments, noticing any sensations of calm, relief, or steadiness as his peace fills you.

You keep him in perfect peace whose mind is stayed on you, because he trusts in you.
— Isaiah 26:3 (ESV)

# THE VINE

**VERSES TO CONSIDER:**

- I am the vine; you are the branches. Whoever abides in me and I in him, he it is that bears much fruit, for apart from me you can do nothing. — John 15:5 (ESV)
- Also see: Galatians 5:22–23; Philippians 4:13

**DEVOTIONAL THOUGHT**

In a world that praises independence, Jesus invites us into something far better: connection. He doesn't say, "Try harder." He says, "Abide in me." We aren't asked to be the vine—just a branch. That one shift changes everything. Branches don't force fruit; they simply stay connected to the source. When we try to live in our own strength, we run dry. But when we remain in Christ, life flows. Strength flows. Peace flows. Fruit grows by connection, not by force.

But abiding isn't passive; it's daily dependence. It's remembering that he's the one who nourishes us, shapes us, and sustains us. We flourish not because of what we do, but because of where we dwell. If you're weary, maybe it's not because you're doing too much—but because you're doing it apart from the Vine. Come back. Rest in him. Life is found in the Source, the True Vine.

**BECAUSE GOD IS THE VINE, I AM...**

...able to flourish when I stay close to him. I am not withered. I am alive and fruitful. Because God is my source, I don't have to strive to produce what only he can.

*The Vine*

# THE VINE

## JOURNALING PROMPTS

- Where have I been trying to bear fruit without staying connected to the Vine?
- Jesus, teach me how to abide in you today. What would it look like to stay with you instead of striving on my own?

## PRACTICING HIS PRESENCE

Take five minutes today to sit in stillness. Picture yourself as a branch connected to the Vine. Breathe deeply, and as you inhale, pray: "You are my source." As you exhale, release your striving.

# THE VINE

REFLECT & RESPOND

Abiding in Christ is always about connection. We are branches, not the Vine. When we stay connected to him, life, strength, and peace flow naturally; fruit grows by grace, not by force.

Branches Connected Exercise
- Stand or sit comfortably.
- Imagine roots growing from your feet deep into the ground, anchoring you.
- Stretch your arms gently upward like branches reaching toward the sky.
- Close your eyes if you like, and take slow, deep breaths.
- With each inhale, picture life from the Vine flowing into you.
- With each exhale, release your striving, tension, and weariness.
- Whisper: "I abide in You, Vine of Life."

Take a few moments here. Let your body feel rooted. Let your spirit rest in the One who nourishes, sustains, and flows through you.

I AM THE *Vine;* O YOU ARE THE *branches*

JOHN 15:5 (ESV)

# JEHOVAH SHAMMAH

**VERSES TO CONSIDER:**

- ...and the name of the city from that time on shall be, The Lord Is There.
  — Ezekiel 48:35 (ESV)
- Also see: Matthew 28:20; Deuteronomy 31:6; 1 Corinthians 6:19

**DEVOTIONAL THOUGHT**

Jehovah Shammah doesn't mean God *was* there—it means God *is* there. His presence is a promise sealed by love, not a reward for spiritual performance. From the temple to the cross to the Holy Spirit within us, God has always made a way to dwell with us.

We tend to look for God in mountaintop moments or miraculous signs, but Jehovah Shammah shows up in our Mondays, our messes, our midnight fears. He is the God who is on hand. He is not distant, delayed, or demanding that we fix ourselves before he draws near. He's in the waiting room, the quiet kitchen, the long stretch of unknown. If we pause and listen, we'll realize: the Lord is here.

**BECAUSE GOD IS JEHOVAH SHAMMAH, I AM...**

...never alone. I don't have to summon him—he's already here. I am not abandoned. I am always accompanied by his presence.

*Jehovah Shammah*

# JEHOVAH SHAMMAH

## JOURNALING PROMPTS

- God, where have I been living like you're far away?
- Thank you for being the God who stays. Show me how to recognize your nearness today.

## PRACTICING HIS PRESENCE

Set a timer for three moments today, such as morning, noon, and evening. At each one, simply pause and whisper, "You are here." Let that truth anchor you. Let it change how you respond, rest, and relate. Note how it changes the day for you.

# JEHOVAH SHAMMAH

REFLECT & RESPOND

God's presence is not bound by our clocks or calendars. Jehovah Shammah is with us in every moment—past, present, and future—because for him, it's all one Eternal Now. When the Bible says he will never leave us or forsake us, it's because he fills all of time, all at once.

Lifeline of Presence Exercise
1. Draw a horizontal line representing your life from childhood through today, and stretching into the future.
2. Mark moments where God revealed his presence—comforting, guiding, protecting, or providing.
3. As you reflect on each point, remember that while we experience time linearly, God experiences it all at once. His "Now" encompasses every joy, pain, and turning point.
4. Whisper a prayer at each point: "Jehovah Shammah, You are here—then, now, and always."
5. Sit quietly at the end of your timeline, letting gratitude for his Eternal Now fill your heart.

# THE LORD IS THERE. — EZEKIEL 48:35

# JEHOVAH TSIDKENU

### VERSES TO CONSIDER:

- ...And this is the name by which He will be called: "The Lord is our righteousness." —Jeremiah 23:6 (ESV)
- God made him who had no sin to be sin for us, so that in him we might become the righteousness of God. —2 Corinthians 5:21
- Also see: Isaiah 61:10; Romans 1:16–17; 1 Corinthians 1:30

### DEVOTIONAL THOUGHT

Righteousness is more than a moral standard—it's a gift. That gift is Jesus. When we fail, when shame whispers that we're not enough, when we feel the weight of trying to be good or holy or worthy, Jehovah Tsidkenu steps in and clothes us with himself. The cross was not just about removing our sin; it was about exchanging it with righteousness, his righteousness.

In Christ, we wear a robe we didn't sew, walk in a freedom we didn't earn, and are called righteous, not because we are without fault, but because he is. Jehovah Tsidkenu reminds us that grace isn't an escape from justice; it's the full satisfaction of justice, given in love. So we no longer live under the pressure to be perfect. We live in the peace of being made right.

### BECAUSE GOD IS JEHOVAH TSIDKENU, I AM...

...not condemned—I am covered. I am not striving; I am standing secure in Christ. Because God is my righteousness, I don't have to earn his approval.

*Jehovah Tsidkenu*

# JEHOVAH TSIDKENU

## JOURNALING PROMPTS

- Where have I been trying to earn what you've already given me?
- Jesus, thank you for trading your righteousness for my sin. Help me live like I'm forgiven.

## PRACTICING HIS PRESENCE

When shame, guilt, or insecurity rises today, place your hand over your heart and quietly say, "I am clothed in Christ. I am righteous in him." Let this truth settle your spirit and shape your decisions.

# JEHOVAH TSIDKENU

REFLECT & RESPOND

Jehovah Tsidkenu—the Lord our Righteousness—reminds us that holiness isn't something we earn; it's something we wear. In Christ, we're no longer striving to be enough; we're resting in the One who is. Each day we "put on" his righteousness, we're choosing to live from grace instead of guilt, from peace instead of pressure.

Getting Dressed Exercise
As you get dressed today, turn each piece of clothing into a quiet declaration of truth:
- As you put on your shirt, say, "I am clothed in Christ's righteousness."
- As you fasten your belt, remember, "His truth holds me together."
- As you slip on your shoes, declare, "I walk in peace, not pressure."
- As you put on your jewelry or accessories, remind yourself, "I am adorned with grace and strength."

Let the act of getting dressed become a daily reminder that you no longer wear shame or striving. You wear Christ's righteousness and in him are complete, accepted, and made right.

IN THE FUTURE THERE IS RESERVED FOR ME THE *crown* OF RIGHTEOUSNESS WHICH THE LORD, THE RIGHTEOUS JUDGE, WILL AWARD TO ME ON THAT DAY; AND NOT ONLY TO ME, BUT ALSO TO ALL WHO *have loved* HIS APPEARING. —2 TIMOTHY 4:8 NASB

# HOLY

### VERSES TO CONSIDER:

- Be holy, for I am holy. — 1 Peter 1:16
- God made him who had no sin to be sin for us, so that in him we might become the righteousness of God. — 2 Corinthians 5:21

### DEVOTIONAL THOUGHT

Holiness has been stolen from us, twisted into something intimidating, punitive, even painful. Many of us flinch at the word because it was used as a weapon, a whip to keep us in line. But "Be holy, for I am holy" is a divine invitation. God is not asking us to climb some impossible mountain of moral perfection; he invites us to dwell with him, in him.

Holiness isn't just moral cleanliness; it's otherness. It's the searing light that exposes our perversity—the craving in us for things that will kill us—and yet it's also the flame that purifies, not to destroy, but to make whole. God is a consuming fire, yes, but his fire is love. Relentless, pursuing, excruciating love that remakes us. His holiness is freedom not only from sin, but to dwell with him. To be made whole. To live full of joy. The entire arc of Scripture beats with this desire: that a holy God might dwell with a holy people. He made a way for that through Jesus. And now, he calls us to dwell together.

### BECAUSE GOD IS HOLY, I AM...

...no longer a slave to the darkness. I am set apart. I belong to him. I am free not just from sin, but to thrive. All this is true for me because God is holy and set apart, and because Jesus exchanged his holiness for my sinfulness.

# HOLY

## JOURNALING PROMPTS

- Where have I associated holiness with fear or shame instead of freedom and joy?
- God, show me what you want to heal in me so that I may dwell more fully in your holy presence.

## PRACTICING HIS PRESENCE

Today, when you feel tempted, unworthy, or overwhelmed, pause and repeat: "You are holy. And in you, I am set apart. I choose to abide in you."

Or, go for a short walk and ask God: "What in me are you lovingly purifying so we can dwell more closely together?"

# HOLY

## REFLECT & RESPOND

Holiness exchanges what is broken in us for God's wholeness. As you wear his truth today, notice the places in your life he has made complete. Let this awareness shape your words, actions, and thoughts, reminding you that in him, you are fully whole.

The Puzzle of You Exercise
- Take a quiet moment at the end of the day to imagine your life as a puzzle. Some pieces feel jagged, missing, or out of place.
- Visualize God holding the missing pieces. His holiness is what completes the picture, making you whole.
- Slowly go through your day, noticing the "gaps" in your thoughts, your heart, or your interactions. With each one, silently say: "Holy Father, you make me whole."
- If helpful, you can write down one piece at a time—an area of brokenness, fear, or weakness—and next to it, write how God's holiness restores it.

Use the illustration on the next page to help you think through the pieces of your day and where God is pulling you together to represent his image here on earth.

# FAITHFUL & TRUE

**VERSES TO CONSIDER:**

- Then I saw heaven opened, and behold, a white horse! The one sitting on it is called Faithful and True... — Revelation 19:11
- Know therefore that the Lord your God is God, the faithful God who keeps covenant and steadfast love... — Deuteronomy 7:9

## DEVOTIONAL THOUGHT

What God says, he always does. He is not like people who forget, fail, or falter. He is the promisor of promises *already fulfilled*. And what he does can never be separated from who he is. He doesn't merely act faithfully; he *is faithful*. Every word from his mouth is backed by the full weight of his eternal, dependable nature. That's why we can trust his promises, not as wishful thinking but as revelations of his unchanging heart.

When we claim his promises, we are not chanting empty incantations—we are declaring who God already has proved he is. We're not trying to get him to do something; we are aligning ourselves with what he's already doing. His faithfulness is not limited to the past or locked away in Scripture. Because God exists fully in the past, present, and future, his words reverberate through time to the future, where his promises are completely fulfilled. That means the promises he made long ago still echo with power today—for you, for now.

## BECAUSE GOD IS FAITHFUL & TRUE, I AM...

...secure in his promises, held by his unchanging nature. I am not foolish for hoping—I am anchored. Because God is Faithful and True, I can trust him repeatedly, especially when I don't yet see the outcome.

*Faithful & True*

# FAITHFUL & TRUE

## JOURNALING PROMPTS

- Where have I struggled to believe that God will keep his promises to me?
- God, remind me of a time you were faithful when I couldn't see the way forward.

## PRACTICING HIS PRESENCE

Today, when anxiety creeps in, whisper: "You are faithful and true. You do not forget me."

Or, take 5 minutes to recall one promise of God from Scripture and how it reflects his heart. Insert your name in the promise. Let that be your anchor for the day.

# FAITHFUL & TRUE

REFLECT & RESPOND

Faithfulness is who God is, not just what he does. Think back over your life: moments of provision, rescue, comfort, or answered prayer. Each one is a thread of his unchanging love, woven through time to remind you that he never forgets his promises. The same God who carried you then is carrying you now.

In the next practice, you'll have the opportunity to create a tangible way to remember those moments and keep his faithfulness close at hand.

String of Remembrance
Before you go on this next exercise, take a few quiet minutes to reflect on moments in your life when God's faithfulness carried you: times when He provided, healed, comforted, or simply stayed when others didn't. Jot down a few of those memories.

Then visit a fabric or craft store and choose beads to represent each one. Maybe a blue bead for peace, a clear one for clarity, a rough-edged one for a hard season redeemed. Let your choices tell your story.

When you get home, string them together into a bracelet, keychain, or small strand you can keep nearby. As you finger each bead, pray:

"God, You were faithful then. You are faithful now. You will be faithful again."

Let each bead be a testimony, each prayer a tangible reminder of trust in God, holding you close to the Faithful and True One

Know therefore that the Lord your God is God, the

FAITHFUL

who keeps covenant and steadfast love...
(Deuteronomy 7:9)

# JEHOVAH M'KADDESH

### VERSES TO CONSIDER:

- You are to speak to the people of Israel and say, "Above all you shall keep my Sabbaths, for this is a sign between me and you throughout your generations, that you may know that I, the Lord, sanctify you." — Exodus 31:13
- ...to those who are elect...in the sanctification of the Spirit, for obedience to Jesus Christ and for sprinkling with his blood... — 1 Peter 1:2

### DEVOTIONAL THOUGHT

Sanctification is a Spirit-led transformation, not a self-improvement project. Jehovah M'Kaddesh, the Lord who sanctifies, is not asking us to become holy in our own strength. He's inviting us to walk with him, to yield, to behold his glory, and be changed.

This isn't instant. We were justified the moment we trusted in Jesus, but now we are *being* sanctified. Made holy. It's a lifelong process. The Holy Spirit exposes sin, reveals truth, and points us to Jesus again and again. We are called to respond, not resist. To surrender, not strive. And in doing so, we don't become better people or better versions of ourselves; we become like him. The Lord who sanctifies doesn't just command holiness—he provides it, forming in us the very character of Christ.

### BECAUSE GOD IS JEHOVAH M'KADDESH, I AM...

...set apart and made holy. I am made holy by his Spirit at work within me, not by my striving. I am being shaped into his likeness, from the inside out.

*Jehovah M'Kaddesh*

# JEHOVAH M'KADDESH

JOURNALING PROMPTS

- Where have I been resisting the Holy Spirit's transforming work in me?
- God, what sin are you gently exposing right now? Help me respond in repentance, not shame.

PRACTICING HIS PRESENCE

When a moment of impatience, anger, or fear arises today, pause and whisper, "Spirit, sanctify me. Make me like Jesus." Let this become your turning point instead of a breaking point.

Or, surrender. Say, "All that I am (the good, the bad, the ugly), all that I am not (the good, the bad, and the ugly), and all that I ever hope to be, I surrender absolutely."

# JEHOVAH M'KADDESH

REFLECT & RESPOND

Jehovah M'Kaddesh doesn't call you to perfect yourself. He calls you to walk with him as he perfects you into the image of Christ. Every surrendered moment becomes sacred ground where his Spirit shapes your heart. As you yield to his refining work, you'll begin to see holiness not as pressure, but as the steady, transforming nearness of the God who sanctifies.

The Refining Bowl
Faithfulness is who God is, not just what He does. Think back over your life—moments of provision, rescue, comfort, or answered prayer. Each one is a thread of his unchanging love, woven through time to remind you that he never forgets his promises. The same God who carried you then is carrying you now.

In the next practice, you'll have the opportunity to create a tangible way to remember those moments and keep his faithfulness close at hand.

Find a small bowl or dish (something simple, even ordinary) and place it somewhere you'll see it often throughout the day. This will become your "refining bowl."

Throughout the day, when you notice moments of impatience, fear, or self-focus, pause and imagine placing that thought, reaction, or burden into the bowl. Silently pray, "Jehovah M'Kaddesh, this is yours. Sanctify me. Make me like Jesus."

At the end of the day, spend a few minutes reflecting on what you've placed there. Notice how surrendering throughout the day made room for peace, gentleness, or clarity to emerge. Sanctification is not about striving to be flawless; it's the quiet, continual yielding that allows the Spirit to refine and reshape us into Christ's likeness—one surrendered moment at a time.

# EL OLAM

### VERSES TO CONSIDER:

- Abraham planted a tamarisk tree in Beersheba and called there on the name of the Lord, the Everlasting God. — Genesis 21:33
- Have you not known? Have you not heard? The Lord is the everlasting God, the Creator of the ends of the earth. He does not faint or grow weary; His understanding is unsearchable. — Isaiah 40:28

### DEVOTIONAL THOUGHT

We are creatures of change, bound by time, aging, and transition. But El Olam is not like us. He is the Everlasting God, uncreated and unchanging, holy from eternity past to eternity future.

Everything in our world eventually shifts: jobs, relationships, seasons, emotions. But El Olam remains constant. His perfection needs no improvement. His holiness cannot diminish. And because we belong to him, we have an anchor for our souls: the One who spans all of history and invites us to live in light of eternity. We are not just part of a moment; we are part of his eternal story.

Because he is everlasting, his love is, too. It does not grow or lessen over time. We cannot earn more of it. He already loved us fully before the world was created. Nothing we do or say can make his love increase or shrink. It is perfect, complete, and forever secure.

### BECAUSE GOD IS EL OLAM, I AM...

Because God is El Olam, I can rest in his unchanging presence. I am loved, I am held, I am never forgotten. Though life on earth is fleeting,
in Christ I am part of his everlasting story.

# EL OLAM

## JOURNALING PROMPTS

- Where am I tempted to place my hope in things that are temporary?
- God, remind me today that you are eternal and unchanging. Help me to rest in your everlasting arms.

## PRACTICING HIS PRESENCE

When something feels uncertain or out of control today, pause and whisper: "You are El Olam—unchanging, eternal, and faithful. I belong to You." Let that truth settle your soul.

Or, when you feel time moving too fast and regret for not making the most of every moment creeps in, remind yourself: "My life on earth is fleeting, yes. But my life in Christ is part of God's everlasting story."

# EL OLAM

REFLECT & RESPOND

Your story is not just a series of moments. It is part of God's eternal narrative. El Olam has been present in your roots, shaping your trunk, and guiding the growth of your branches so you can become a "tree planted by the streams of waters" (Psalm 1). Even when life feels fleeting or uncertain, you are held by the Everlasting One. Pause and let that truth settle in your heart: your past, present, and future belong to him, and nothing can separate you from his unchanging love.

Eternal Story Tree
Take a piece of paper and draw a simple tree, or use the one on the next page to outline the following.
- Roots: Reflect on your origins: family, community, experiences, and formative moments. Recognize how God's presence has been there, even in ways you didn't notice at the time.
- Trunk and Ground: Represent your current life. Where are you rooted today? How is God sustaining you in the present?
- Branches: Represent your hopes, dreams, and the legacy you wish to leave. Imagine how God, the Everlasting One, is weaving these into His eternal story.

As you complete the tree, pause and whisper: "El Olam, my story is in Your hands, from beginning to eternity. I belong to You."

# JEHOVAH QANNA

### VERSES TO CONSIDER:

- For you shall worship no other god, for the Lord, whose name is Jealous, is a jealous God. – Exodus 34:14
- You shall not bow down to them or serve them, for I the Lord your God am a jealous God… – Deuteronomy 5:9a

### DEVOTIONAL THOUGHT

God's jealousy is not petty or insecure, but instead pure, holy, and protective. Jehovah Qanna, the God who is a jealous God, doesn't compete for our affection because he needs us, but because he made us for himself. He knows that every false god—every idol we chase—is a perversion that leads to our destruction. So when his heart burns with jealousy, it is not to control us, but to rescue us from lesser loves that will ultimately destroy us.

This means his jealousy is a measure of our worth to him. It is a sign of how fiercely he loves us, how relentlessly he desires for us to thrive, and how committed he is to keeping our hearts from harm. He's not content to share our devotion with things that cannot satisfy because he knows he is the only One who can satisfy! When we turn to him, we find a love that doesn't use us, abandon us, or manipulate us but fiercely, faithfully pursues us for our good.

### BECAUSE GOD IS JEHOVAH QANNA, I AM…

…deeply loved, pursued, and protected. I am not disposable. On the contrary, I am desired. His fierce devotion means I am never overlooked. He moves heaven and earth to win me to himself.

*Jehovah Qanna*

# JEHOVAH QANNA

## JOURNALING PROMPTS

- Where have I been giving my affection or trust to something other than God?
- God, what idols have I mistaken for good that you're jealous to free me from?

## PRACTICING HIS PRESENCE

When you feel drawn toward something that promises quick comfort or identity, pause and whisper: "You, Lord, are jealous for me. Help me return to you."

Light a candle today as a symbol of God's consuming love and his jealousy not to destroy you, but to draw you fully into his presence.

# JEHOVAH QANNA

REFLECT & RESPOND

God's jealousy is a sign of his fierce love for you. He does not compete out of insecurity, but out of care, by protecting your heart from what cannot satisfy. Take a moment to notice areas where you've relied on lesser loves, and invite him to reclaim those areas.

As you reflect, remind yourself: the battles you feel alone in are already his to fight. Trust that the God who fiercely desires your flourishing is both relentless and tender. Let this awareness shape how you spend your time, energy, and devotion today, choosing what truly satisfies: Him.

Naming The Idols
Take a few quiet minutes to reflect on the things or habits that compete for your heart, which are anything that pulls your trust, affection, or energy away from God. These could be work, approval, worry, or even routines that distract you from intimacy with him.

Write each one down on a small piece of paper or in your journal. As you do, whisper or declare: "Jehovah Qanna, guard my heart. I choose You above all else."

Then, take a moment to lift your hands and let God symbolically remove these idols from your life, trusting that his protective, jealous love is keeping you safe. Close by thanking him for fiercely pursuing you and for the deep satisfaction only he can provide.

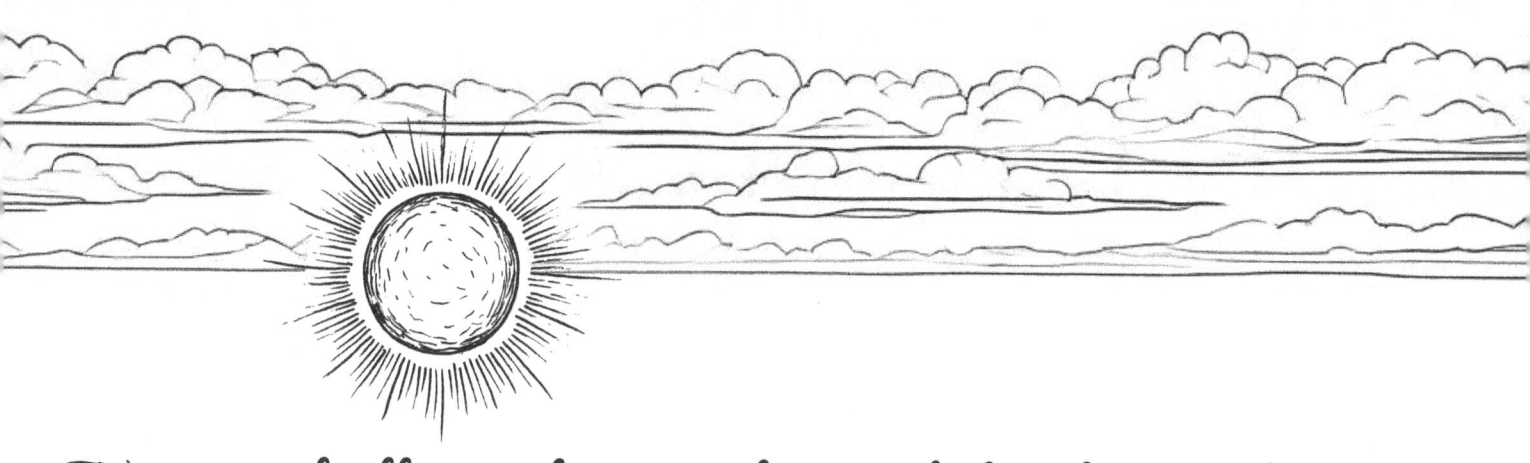

For you shall worship no other god, for the Lord, whose name is Jealous, is a jealous God. – Exodus 34:14

# JEHOVAH CHERUB

**VERSES TO CONSIDER:**

- The Lord will fight for you; you need only to be still. — Exodus 14:14
- This is what the Lord says to you: "Do not be afraid or discouraged because of this vast army. For the battle is not yours, but God's." — 2 Chronicles 20:15b

**DEVOTIONAL THOUGHT**

Jehovah Cherub means "The Lord our Sword." It's not a fat little baby angel. It's a mighty God who doesn't just fight beside us in battle—*he is the weapon.* He flies into the storm on our behalf, sword drawn, thundering from the heavens. The image is wild, majestic, and deeply personal. We are not just survivors…the God of Angel Armies fights for us!

Sometimes our battles feel invisible. Fear. Shame. Exhaustion. Doubt. These are enemies we cannot touch but feel every day. But the battle is the Lord's. He doesn't wait for us to get stronger. He steps into the chaos while we're still trembling and takes the fight as his own. Our job is to stand firm in trust, knowing that the God who has proven faithful for all eternity will continue to be faithful for all eternity. The war has already been decided, and we are held by the One who never loses.

**BECAUSE GOD IS JEHOVAH CHERUB, I AM…**

…not defenseless. I am covered, protected, and fought for. I don't have to win every battle—he already has.

*Jehovah Cherub*

# JEHOVAH CHERUB

## JOURNALING PROMPTS

- God, where am I trying to fight in my own strength instead of trusting you to be my sword?
- What battle feels too big for me right now? Speak the truth over it.

## PRACTICING HIS PRESENCE

Pause today whenever anxiety rises and whisper: "Jehovah Cherub, fight for me. I trust You with this battle.

Or, stand still for one minute with your hands open. Let this physical posture remind you the battle is not yours to carry alone.

# JEHOVAH CHERUB

REFLECT & RESPOND

Jehovah Cherub reminds us that we are not left to face our battles alone. Fear, doubt, shame, and exhaustion are real, but they do not have the final word. Pause and consider the areas of your life where you've tried to fight alone. Invite God to step in as your Sword, taking up the battle on your behalf.

Stand in stillness and trust that the victory has already been decided. Let this truth reshape your thoughts and actions today, knowing that you are held by a mighty God whose victory is certain and whose power is at work in your life.

Walking With The Sword
1. Identify your battle areas: Begin by listing the struggles, fears, or pressures weighing on you this week. These could be internal (anxiety, doubt, shame) or external (conflicts, responsibilities, overwhelming tasks).
2. Visualize God as your sword: Imagine Jehovah Cherub standing before you, sword drawn, ready to fight on your behalf. Picture the chaos of your challenges being met and overcome by his power and not by your own strength.
3. Physical posture: Carry your Bible as the sword of the Holy Spirit. Speak a declaration such as: "Jehovah Cherub, fight for me. I trust You with this battle."
4. Prayer walk: Step outside or around your space and take a slow, intentional walk. With each step, hand over specific struggles to God. Pray aloud or silently for his protection, guidance, and victory over each area of your life. Imagine his sword moving ahead of you or swinging the Bible in front of you, as if clearing the path.
5. Anchor for the day: Repeat this activity and declaration anytime anxiety, fear, or pressure rises. Allow your mind and body to remember that the battle belongs to the Lord and that you walk in his power and peace.

"Do not be afraid or discouraged...For *the battle is not yours* but God's. — 2 Chronicles 20:15b

# JEHOVAH GO'EL

### VERSES TO CONSIDER:

- Do not be afraid, you worm Jacob, little Israel, do not fear, for I myself will help you, declares the Lord, your Redeemer, the Holy One of Israel. — Isaiah 41:14
- You are not your own; you were bought at a price. Therefore honor God with your bodies. — 1 Corinthians 6:19b–20

### DEVOTIONAL THOUGHT

Jehovah Go'el is the Kinsman-Redeemer: the One who has both the right and the love to buy us back from bondage. In biblical times, a redeemer was usually a close relative who stepped in to restore what had been lost: freedom, family, land, or legacy. It was personal, costly, and motivated by covenantal love.

That's exactly what God did for us. He didn't wait for the Year of Jubilee; he came himself. When we had sold ourselves into sin—into perversion, addiction, despair—he didn't leave us to rot. Jesus, our perfect Redeemer, paid the full price with his own blood. He took our shame, our debt, our exile, and brought us back into our inheritance...him. We are his twice over: first by creation, then by redemption. That's why we honor him with our whole lives. We do not do this to earn his love or favor, but because we already belong to him. We're not trying to prove our value—we're living from it.

### BECAUSE GOD IS JEHOVAH GO'EL, I AM...

...not forgotten or forsaken. I am deeply known, bought back at great cost, and fully his. My worth isn't defined by my failures but by the price he paid to rescue me.

*Jehovah Go'el*

# JEHOVAH GO'EL

JOURNALING PROMPTS

- God, where have I been living like I still belong to my old ways?
- Jesus, thank you for redeeming me when I had nothing to offer. Help me live like I'm truly yours.

## PRACTICING HIS PRESENCE

Today, when you're tempted to believe you're worthless or stuck in the past, pause and whisper: "I am redeemed. I belong to you."

Or, as you get dressed, say aloud: "This body is not my own. It was bought with a heavy price. I honor you with it today."

# JEHOVAH GO'EL

REFLECT & RESPOND

Jehovah Go'el reminds us that redemption is a free gift we receive. He steps into the bondage we deserve, pays the full price, and calls us his own. Pause and consider the places in your life where you still live as though you are unredeemed or unworthy.

Invite your Kinsman-Redeemer to reclaim what has been lost, such as your peace, purpose, and joy. Let his ownership free you from striving, and rest in the truth that you are already bought back, fully loved, and forever his.

Reclaimed & Restored
1. Find an old or discarded item around your home—something worn, forgotten, or in need of care. It could be a piece of jewelry to polish, a torn page to mend, or a plant to re-pot. As you restore it, reflect on how your Redeemer has done the same with you.
2. Whisper a prayer of gratitude: "Jehovah Go'el, thank You for reclaiming me. Nothing in my life is too broken for You to redeem."
3. Let this act of restoration remind you that his redemption reaches into the smallest corners of your life, making all things new.

You are not your own; you were redeemed at a price. Therefore honor God with your bodies.
— 1 Corinthians 6:19b-20

# JEHOVAH HAMELECH

### VERSES TO CONSIDER:

- Shout joyfully before the Lord, the King. — Psalm 98:6
- The Lord is King forever and ever; the nations perish from his land. — Psalm 10:16

### DEVOTIONAL THOUGHT

Jehovah Hamelech means "The Lord, my King." He is not just a king; he is *the King*—ruling with power, justice, and mercy. But unlike earthly kings who take power for themselves, Jehovah Hamelech gave himself to win us to himself. He reigns from a cross before he returns with a crown. His Kingdom flips every earthly system: the greatest is the servant, the poor are blessed, the meek inherit the earth.

And here's another wonder: we are not only his citizens, we are his family, children of the King. We live under his rule, yes—but we also dine at his table. He governs our lives not by domination, but by redemption. To belong to Jehovah Hamelech is to submit and be secure, to bow and be lifted, to obey and be fully free.

And he is not a temporary ruler. A related name, Jehovah Malech-Olam, means "The Lord Who Is King Forever." When the world around us crumbles—when governments shift, leaders fail, systems disappoint—God's reign is unshakable. His justice never wavers. His mercy never expires. When we root our identity in this Kingdom, we gain a security no earthly power can give and no earthly chaos can take away.

### BECAUSE GOD IS JEHOVAH HAMELECH, I AM…

…not subject to the chaos of this world. I am ruled by perfect love, anchored in eternal authority, and seated at the table of the King.

*Jehovah Hamelech*

# JEHOVAH HAMELECH

## JOURNALING PROMPTS

- Where am I resisting the Lord's rule in my life?
- Jesus, show me where I've trusted in earthly power instead of your eternal Kingdom.
- What would change if I really believed I am a child of the King?

## PRACTICING HIS PRESENCE

When you feel overwhelmed by the world's noise or instability, pause and repeat: "You are King forever. I belong to your Kingdom."

Or, as you go about your day, look for small ways to serve others as royalty in God's upside-down Kingdom.

# JEHOVAH HAMELECH

REFLECT & RESPOND

Jehovah Hamelech invites us to live as those ruled not by fear or chaos, but by a King whose authority is love. Pause and consider: where in your life are you still trying to rule your own kingdom? What areas feel unsettled because you've been holding the crown?

Surrender them to the Lord who reigns forever. Let his sovereignty bring stillness to your striving. As you go about your day, walk with the quiet dignity of one who belongs to a Kingdom that cannot be shaken, serving others not from obligation, but from royal identity.

Living Under the Reign of the King
When life feels uncertain or self-focused, our perspective can shrink to our own little kingdoms—our worries, goals, and control. This exercise helps reorient your heart to the reign of Jehovah Hamelech, the true King.

How it works:
1. Name your kingdom moments: At the end of the day, write down three moments where you felt tempted to rule your own life or to control, fix, or elevate yourself.
2. Reframe them under his reign: Next to each one, declare, "You are King here." Offer those moments back to him in trust.
3. Respond with gratitude: Write one way his rule brings peace, justice, or mercy into that area of your life.
4. Over time, this practice shifts your focus from self-rule to divine rule, reminding you that real freedom is found in surrender to the King who reigns forever.

# JEHOVAH HASHOPET

### VERSES TO CONSIDER:

- I have not wronged you, but you are doing me wrong by waging war against me. Let the Lord, the Judge, decide the dispute this day between the Israelites and the Ammonites. — Judges 11:27
- God is a righteous judge, a God who displays his wrath every day. — Psalm 7:11

### DEVOTIONAL THOUGHT

Jehovah Hashopet means The Lord, the Judge. He is not a corrupt or distant authority figure; he is holy, impartial, and just. He presides over a heavenly court, as described in Revelation, where thrones surround his throne, and multitudes testify to his righteousness. Nothing escapes his notice, not even what is whispered in secret. He alone sees the heart and weighs the motives no one else can perceive.

This truth should stir both reverence and relief. Because God judges rightly, I can rest knowing that evil will not win and righteousness will not be ignored—not in this world, and not in me. But the weight of that justice would crush us if not for Jesus. In Christ, the Judge becomes our Justifier (Romans 3:26). The gavel of heaven, which could rightly fall on us, fell on him. Now, instead of fear, we receive grace. Instead of condemnation, we enter the plea: covered by the blood of Jesus. Then we hear the astonishing verdict: not guilty. To walk with Jehovah Hashopet is to live with both reverence and freedom that comes from knowing the cost the Judge paid.

### BECAUSE GOD IS JEHOVAH HASHOPET, I AM...

...accountable—but not condemned. I stand before him with awe, but in Christ, I also stand unashamed. I am justified, not by my merit, but by his mercy.

*Jehovah Hashopet*

# JEHOVAH HASHOPET

## JOURNALING PROMPTS

- God, where have I stopped treating Your word as authoritative in my life?
- What would it look like to live today in light of the truth that You are my Judge and my Justifier?

## PRACTICING HIS PRESENCE

When you feel tempted to justify your actions to others, pause and whisper: "You, Lord, are my Judge. You see me fully, and I belong to you."

Or, sit quietly for 3–5 minutes and imagine standing before God's throne, then let Scripture remind you that, in Christ, you are covered and accepted. Listen to what God declares about you.

# JEHOVAH HASHOPET

REFLECT & RESPOND

Jehovah Hashopet reminds us that we are seen, known, and perfectly judged by the righteousness of Christ, not by our own merit. Pause and consider: where in your life have you carried shame, fear, or doubt, thinking the verdict might fall against you?

Bring those areas before the Judge and hear His declaration: Not guilty. Covered by the blood of Jesus. Only God's perfect justice could leave mercy and peace in its wake. Let this truth reshape your thoughts and actions today, walking in the freedom and acceptance that only God's justice can provide.

Courtroom of Heaven
- Settle into a quiet space – Sit comfortably and take several deep breaths, imagining yourself entering a grand courtroom. The Judge is Christ, radiant with holiness and justice. The Holy Spirit is present as your advocate, standing with you.
- Present your case – Bring to mind the areas of your life where you've carried shame, fear, guilt, or doubt. Imagine placing each one on the table before the Judge. Speak honestly, knowing the Spirit intercedes on your behalf.
- Hear the verdict – Listen as the Judge declares over each situation: "Not guilty. Covered by the blood of Jesus Christ. You are accepted, righteous, and free." Let each declaration wash over you, affirming God's justice and grace.
- Reflect – Take a moment to consider how your thoughts, actions, or emotions might change now that these areas are fully redeemed and accepted in Christ.
- Close in gratitude – Thank God for his perfect judgment, for Christ's sacrifice that covers you, and for the Holy Spirit who advocates on your behalf. Carry this sense of freedom into your day.

# JEHOVAH KHABODI

### VERSES TO CONSIDER:

- But you, O Lord, are a shield about me, my glory, and the lifter of my head. —Psalm 3:3
- And we all, who with unveiled faces contemplate the Lord's glory, are being transformed into his image with ever-increasing glory...—2 Corinthians 3:18

### DEVOTIONAL THOUGHT

Jehovah Khabodi means The Lord, my Glory. This name reflects the radiant majesty of God—and the miraculous truth that his glory is not just in heaven, it covers us here. It lifts us. It restores us. In Psalm 3, David, surrounded by enemies and accusations, says, "You, O Lord, are…my glory, and the lifter of my head." In moments of humiliation, loss, or despair, God lifts us with honor. He re-establishes our worth in him.

Throughout the Old Testament, God's glory appeared in power: in a cloud by day, fire by night, filling the temple while people fell in shock, and blazing in Ezekiel's vision. Moses longed to see it, and God allowed a glimpse from the cleft of the rock (Exodus 33:20–22).

But now, in Christ, "the radiance of God's glory" is no longer veiled. Jesus embodies all of God's brilliance and holiness, and through him, we not only witness glory—we carry it. Through the Spirit, we are being transformed to reflect that same glory (2 Corinthians 3:18). God doesn't just shine on us; he shines through us.

### BECAUSE GOD IS JEHOVAH KHABODI, I AM…

…no longer living under shame. I am covered, seen, and honored not by human standards, but by God's love. He lifts my head and restores my dignity.

# JEHOVAH KHABODI

## JOURNALING PROMPTS

- Lord, where have I incorrectly looked for my worth in the opinions of others instead of in your glory?
- Jesus, you are my glory. Show me the places in my life you want to lift and restore.

..................................................................................................................................
..................................................................................................................................
..................................................................................................................................
..................................................................................................................................
..................................................................................................................................
..................................................................................................................................
..................................................................................................................................
..................................................................................................................................

## PRACTICING HIS PRESENCE

Today, when you feel discouraged, whisper: "You are the lifter of my head."

Or, step outside and lift your face to the light, even for a moment. Let it remind you: God's glory covers you and calls you higher. Ask him, "How can I reflect your glory today?"

# JEHOVAH KHABODI

REFLECT & RESPOND

Jehovah Khabodi reminds us that our worth and honor are not defined by circumstances, opinions, or setbacks. Pause and consider: where in your life do you feel diminished, overlooked, or weighed down by others' expectations?

Bring those places before the Lord, the One who is your glory and the lifter of your head. Let his radiance restore your confidence, re-establish your worth, and empower you to reflect his brilliance to the world around you today.

Reflecting God's Glory

- Find a Mirror or a Window: Stand where you can see your reflection or look out into the light. Take a few deep breaths and notice your body, your face, your presence.
- Speak Truth Aloud: Whisper or say confidently: "I am seen by the God who lifts my head. I carry his glory, and his radiance shines through me."
- Identify Your Areas of Discouragement: Take 2–3 minutes to silently acknowledge places you feel unseen, criticized, or diminished. For each, imagine God's glory gently covering it, lifting and restoring it.
- Action Reflection: Think of one practical way you can reflect his glory today, such as words, acts of service, encouragement, or simply carrying yourself with the confidence that comes from being honored by God.
- Close with Gratitude: End by saying, "Thank You, Lord, for making me radiant with Your glory. Let me carry it into every part of my day."

This simple exercise trains your heart to recognize that God's glory is both over you and flowing through you, reshaping how you see yourself and others.

But you, O Lord, are a shield about me, *my glory* and the lifter of my head. —Psalm 3:3

# JEHOVAH MACHSI

### VERSES TO CONSIDER:

- I will say of the Lord, He is my refuge and my fortress: my God; in him will I trust. — Psalm 91:2
- The Lord is my rock, and my fortress, and my deliverer; my God, my strength, in whom I will trust; my buckler, and the horn of my salvation, and my high tower. — Psalm 18:2

### DEVOTIONAL THOUGHT

Jehovah Machsi means The Lord, My Refuge, which is a name that causes us to breathe in comfort. In Psalm 91, we see this name surrounded by promises of protection, rescue, and shelter. Refuge implies more than safety; it means nearness. God doesn't offer a shelter from afar—he is the shelter. His presence is our hiding place.

But this refuge isn't just about surviving the storm. In Psalm 18, David takes it further by calling God Jehovah Misqabbi—My Strong Tower. In ancient times, a high tower was not just a shield from attack; it also offered perspective. From it, you could see the battlefield clearly. That's what God does for us. He lifts us above our circumstances so we see with his eyes. He strengthens our hearts and restores our peace so we can thrive.

When life feels chaotic, painful, or out of control, we don't have to run in fear. We get to run to him. And when we do, we find that Jehovah Machsi doesn't just guard us; Jehovah Misqabbi also lifts us. He becomes our place of stillness and our point of view.

### BECAUSE GOD IS JEHOVAH MACHSI, I AM...

...safe. I am not exposed or defenseless—I am protected, lifted, and held in perfect peace.

*Jehovah Machsi*

# JEHOVAH MACHSI

## JOURNALING PROMPTS

- Lord, what have I been trying to face alone that you're inviting me to bring under your shelter?
- God, help me trade panic for peace by running to you first.

## PRACTICING HIS PRESENCE

When anxiety rises, pause and pray: "You are my refuge and strong tower. I am safe in you."

Or, picture yourself in a high tower, looking out with clarity and calm. Ask God: "What do you see that I don't?"

# JEHOVAH MACHSI

REFLECT & RESPOND

Jehovah Machsi reminds us that we are not left to navigate life's storms alone. Pause and consider: where in your life are you carrying fear, anxiety, or confusion as if you must face it all yourself?

Bring those situations before the Lord, your refuge and strong tower. Let Him lift you above the chaos, give you clarity, and provide the perspective only He can offer. Carry that sense of peace and safety into your day, trusting that you are secure in his presence.

Seeking Refuge In God's Tower
- Create Your Safe Space: Find a quiet spot at home where you can sit or stand without interruption. Imagine it as a personal "tower," a place of perspective and safety.
- Visualize the Tower: Close your eyes and picture yourself rising above the chaos of your day. See life's challenges like a battlefield below, while God lifts you to a vantage point of clarity and peace.
- Prayerful Reflection: Whisper or say aloud:
- "You are my refuge, my strong tower. I am safe in you."
- "From this height, I trust your perspective more than my own."
- Identify What Needs Clarity: Bring to mind areas of anxiety, fear, or uncertainty. Ask God: "What do you see that I don't?" Listen quietly for his guidance, impressions, or peace.
- Anchor in God's Presence: End the exercise by taking 3–5 slow breaths, feeling yourself "anchored" in his refuge. Carry the sense of perspective and calm into the rest of your day. Return whenever necessary.

I WILL SAY OF THE LORD, HE IS

*my refuge and my fortress*

MY GOD; IN HIM WILL I TRUST. — PSALM 91:2

# JEHOVAH 'ORI

### VERSES TO CONSIDER:

- The Lord is my light and my salvation—whom shall I fear?—Psalm 27:1
- I am the light of the world. Whoever follows me will never walk in darkness, but will have the light of life.—John 8:12

### DEVOTIONAL THOUGHT

Jehovah 'Ori—The Lord, My Light—is the name that dispels every shadow. When David declared in Psalm 27:1 that the Lord was his light, he wasn't just using poetic language. He was proclaiming a spiritual reality: in God, there is no darkness. No confusion, no fear, no deception can remain when his presence is near. The light of God confronts, reveals, and leads us out of darkness toward his rescue.

Jesus, the Light of the world, said those who follow him will never walk in darkness. He illuminates the truth. He exposes hidden sin and hidden lies. He gives us direction when we can't see the next step. The light of God is both gentle and fierce—he lights our path (Psalm 119:105) but also scours every dark corner of our hearts (1 John 1:5–9). Jehovah 'Ori reveals what is real. In a world of confusion and mixed messages, his light must be our compass. It shows us who he is, who we are, and where we're going.

And what's more, he calls us to be carriers of his light. Jesus says we are the light of the world—a city on a hill, meant to shine. So today, we don't just bask in the light of Jehovah 'Ori, we carry it boldly, so the world may see and glorify him.

### BECAUSE GOD IS JEHOVAH 'ORI, I AM...

...safe. I am not exposed or defenseless. I am protected, lifted, and held in perfect peace.

# JEHOVAH 'ORI

## JOURNALING PROMPTS

- Lord, is there any area of my life I'm keeping in the dark—something you want to bring into the light?
- God, where do I need your light to guide me right now? What direction am I asking you to clarify?

## PRACTICING HIS PRESENCE

As you become disturbed by corruption in the news or confusion on what is real or a conspiracy, pray: Lord, let that which is hidden be revealed. Deeds done in darkness brought to light—in my own heart and in this world—so that your glory can fill the whole earth.

# JEHOVAH 'ORI

## REFLECT & RESPOND

Jehovah 'Ori reminds us that we are never left in darkness, and that his light exposes what needs to be seen so we can walk in truth. Pause and consider: where in your life or heart are shadows clouding your vision?

Bring those places into the light of the Lord, trusting him to reveal what is real and to guide your next steps. Let his Spirit illuminate and reshape your thoughts, actions, and decisions today, and consider how you might reflect that light to others, becoming a carrier of his truth and glory in a world that needs it.

Mapping God's Light
Materials Needed: Paper and pen (or a notebook), a quiet space with a lamp or natural sunlight.

- Set the Scene: Find a quiet spot and turn on a lamp or sit where sunlight is coming in. Let the physical light remind you of the spiritual light of God.
- Identify the Shadows: On your paper, draw or list the areas of your life where you feel confusion, fear, or darkness. These could be emotions, thoughts, situations, or relationships.
- Illuminate Each Area: Next to each "shadow," write a truth from God's Word, or a promise of his guidance and presence. For example:

  - Shadow: Fear of the future → Light: "The Lord is my light and my salvation" (Psalm 27:1).
  - Shadow: Doubt about my decisions → Light: "Your word is a lamp to my feet and a light to my path" (Psalm 119:105).

- Pray Over Each Area: Whisper or speak aloud a short prayer for each area, inviting God to shine his light and reveal what needs clarity.
- Reflect and Record: At the bottom of your page, write how it feels to bring these shadows into the light. Ask God to show you practical steps to walk in his illumination.

I AM THE LIGHT OF THE WORLD. WHOEVER FOLLOWS ME WILL

*never walk in darkness*

BUT WILL HAVE THE LIGHT OF LIFE. — JOHN 8:12

# JEHOVAH SEL'I

### VERSES TO CONSIDER:

- The Lord is my rock, my fortress and my deliverer; my God is my rock, in whom I take refuge. — Psalm 18:2
- ...they drank from the spiritual rock that accompanied them, and that rock was Christ. — 1 Corinthians 10:4

### DEVOTIONAL THOUGHT

Jehovah Sel'i, meaning The Lord, My Rock, is the unshifting strength beneath our feet. He is not only a place of refuge but the immovable foundation of our lives. David, who lived through caves, conflict, and kingship, didn't call God his rock lightly. He had seen what it meant to be grounded when everything else felt unstable.

Rocks in Scripture are symbolic. In Exodus, God tells Moses to strike the rock, and living water gushes forth to sustain a thirsty people (Exodus 17:6). Paul later tells us this rock was Christ (1 Corinthians 10:4). That means Jehovah Sel'i isn't just a fortress—he's also our source of life. And just as David slung a stone to defeat Goliath, the Rock of our salvation not only grounds us but becomes the weapon that defeats our enemies and launches us into purpose.

When the winds of this world howl and foundations crack, Jehovah Sel'i remains. He doesn't erode. He doesn't fracture. He won't fail under the pressure of your pain. He is the cornerstone (Isaiah 28:16), the firm and tested stone we build our lives on.

### BECAUSE GOD IS JEHOVAH SEL'I, I AM...

...anchored and unshakable. I am not easily moved by storms, trials, or fear. I stand secure, built on his strength and sustained by his life.

*Jehovah Sel'i*

# JEHOVAH SEL'I

## JOURNALING PROMPTS

- God, where have I been trying to build on something other than you?
- Show me any shaky ground I've been standing on—and help me return to the Rock.

## PRACTICING HIS PRESENCE

Stand barefoot on solid ground or a stone path today and whisper, "You are my rock, Jehovah Sel'i—I will not be moved."

Or, when uncertainty rises, pause and declare: "I am anchored in you. You are the immovable foundation beneath my feet."

# JEHOVAH SEL'I

REFLECT & RESPOND

Jehovah Sel'i reminds us that our stability and strength do not come from our circumstances or our own efforts. Instead, they come from the unshakable Rock beneath our feet. Pause and consider: where in your life have you felt unstable, fearful, or on shifting ground?

Bring those places before God and acknowledge him as your foundation. Let the truth that he is immovable shape your thoughts, your decisions, and your confidence today. Stand firm, knowing that when you build on him, you cannot be shaken.

Building On The Rock
Materials Needed: Smooth stones or rocks (river rocks work well), acrylic paint or paint pens, a permanent marker, optional small tray or display area.

1. Select Your Rocks: Choose a few rocks that feel solid and grounded in your hand. These will represent areas of your life—challenges, fears, hopes, or personal strengths.
2. Reflect on God as Your Rock: Take a moment to think about the areas in your life that feel unstable or uncertain. Whisper a prayer like:
   - "Jehovah Sel'i, you are my rock in this situation."
   - "You are my foundation when I feel unsteady."

3. Paint or Write Your Declaration: On each rock, write a word or short phrase that reflects God's strength and faithfulness, like "Strength," "Peace," "Protection," or "I am grounded in You."
4. Place Your Rocks: Arrange your painted rocks in a small display or carry one with you as a reminder that God is the immovable foundation beneath your feet. Each time you see or touch it, whisper your personal declaration of trust in him.

The Lord is my rock, my fortress my fortress and my deliverer my God is my rock, in whom I take refuge. — Psalm 18:2

# JEHOVAH UZZI

### VERSES TO CONSIDER:

- The Lord is my strength and my shield; my heart trusts in him, and I am helped. — Psalm 28:7
- My grace is sufficient for you, for My power is made perfect in weakness. — 2 Corinthians 12:9

### DEVOTIONAL THOUGHT

Jehovah Uzzi is not just a source of strength; he *is* your strength. There's a vast difference. When the burden is too heavy, when the battle too fierce, when your reserves have run dry, he doesn't hand you strength like a tool. Jehovah Uzzi becomes strength within you.

David sang of Jehovah Uzzi after years of running, fighting, and barely holding on. And yet, when the dust settled, he didn't attribute his victory to strategy or stamina. He praised the God who had been his strength through it all (2 Samuel 22:33). Similarly, Paul, exhausted and pleading for relief, heard the Spirit whisper, "My power is made perfect in weakness" (2 Corinthians 12:9). That promise was enough for him and it is enough for us.

God's strength doesn't just sustain us; it transforms us. It moves us to praise when we want to quit. It empowers a righteousness we could never muster on our own. And it gives us a holy confidence that whatever battles lie ahead, the One who empowers us is already victorious. When we are too weak to stand, he stands in us. When we fall, he lifts. Because Jehovah Uzzi is not distant. He is near. He is yours.

### BECAUSE GOD IS JEHOVAH UZZI, I AM…

…not self-made. I am God-sustained. His strength fills my weakness and enables my endurance.

# JEHOVAH UZZI

## JOURNALING PROMPTS

- God, where am I relying on my own strength instead of yours?
- Jesus, help me trade my weariness for your strength today.

## PRACTICING HIS PRESENCE

When you feel overwhelmed, place your hand over your heart and say, "You are my strength, Jehovah Uzzi. I rest in you."

Or, take 5 slow, deep breaths and with each exhale, let go of what you're carrying. Whisper, "Not by my might, but by your Spirit."

# JEHOVAH UZZI

REFLECT & RESPOND

Jehovah Uzzi reminds us that we are not meant to rely on our own strength. Pause and consider: where in your life are you trying to carry burdens that feel too heavy, or face challenges that seem beyond your capacity?

Bring those areas before God and acknowledge him as your strength. Let his power and wisdom, not yours, guide your steps, shape your decisions, and sustain your spirit today. Trust that when you are weak, he is strong within you, and allow that truth to transform both your perspective and your actions.

Open-Handed Strenth

Clench Your Fists – Acknowledge Your Weakness

- Sit or stand comfortably. As feelings of weakness, overwhelm, or fear rise, clench your fists tightly. Name the burden aloud or in your heart: "I am struggling with _____." Feel the tension, recognizing your human limits.

Open Your Palms Upward – Invite God's Strength

- Slowly turn your hands upward, releasing the tension in your fists. Whisper or pray: "Jehovah Uzzi, be my strength. Fill me with your power." Visualize God's strength flowing into you with each breath.

Turn Your Palms Downward – Release Control

- Lower your hands, palms facing down. As you do, say: "Not by my might, but by your Spirit, I am strong." Let go of the need to carry the burden alone, trusting Him to sustain and empower you.

Take Up Space

- Stand and stretch your arms overhead or take a few steps, keeping the affirmation in your heart: "Jehovah Uzzi is my strength." Feel the physical and spiritual release as you move.

This exercise connects your body, breath, and spirit, helping you embody the truth that God's strength is yours to receive and rely upon.

THE LORD IS MY STRENGTH AND MY SHIELD; MY HEART TRUSTS IN HIM, AND I AM HELPED. — PSALM 28:7

# JEHOVAH MAGEN

### VERSES TO CONSIDER:

- Happy are you, O Israel! Who is like you, a people saved by the Lord, the shield of your help and the sword of your triumph! — Deuteronomy 33:29
- Our soul waits for the Lord; he is our help and our shield. — Psalm 33:20
- Above all, taking the shield of faith, with which you will be able to quench all the fiery darts of the wicked one. — Ephesians 6:16

### DEVOTIONAL THOUGHT

Jehovah Magen isn't just a name—it's a reality for those who walk with God becuase they have proved this to themselves. In ancient times, the shield wasn't optional in battle. When David sang of God as his shield, he wasn't offering a poetic metaphor, he was testifying to his own survival.

In our daily battles against anxiety, temptation, opposition, or the inner war of discouragement, God's shield doesn't just cover us passively. Scripture describes both a large shield of total coverage and a buckler, small and wielded offensively. The image is of God surrounding us on every side and simultaneously equipping us for close combat. Even the fiery arrows that could pierce us bounce off when we hold fast to faith in him.

You don't have to manufacture your own defense; let him be the defense you need. He is the shield over your head, the guard at your back, and the force that lets you keep walking forward.

### BECAUSE GOD IS JEHOVAH MAGEN, I AM...

...not exposed, not vulnerable, not unarmed. I am covered—defended on all sides by his faithful protection. Because God is my shield, I don't walk into life unprotected.

*Jehovah Magen*

# JEHOVAH MAGEN

## JOURNALING PROMPTS

- Lord, where have I been trying to protect myself in my own strength instead of trusting you as my shield?
- God, show me the places where I've stepped into battle unarmed. Help me take up the shield of faith again.

........................................................................................................................................

........................................................................................................................................

........................................................................................................................................

........................................................................................................................................

........................................................................................................................................

........................................................................................................................................

........................................................................................................................................

## PRACTICING HIS PRESENCE

Today, when something comes at you unexpectedly—criticism, bad news, worry—pause and say: "You are my shield, Lord. I'm covered."

Or, take a quiet moment and picture yourself surrounded—front, back, sides—by God's presence. Thank him for shielding you in ways you've seen and ways you haven't."

# JEHOVAH MAGEN

REFLECT & RESPOND

Jehovah Magen reminds us that we are never facing life's battles alone. Pause and consider: where have you felt exposed, vulnerable, or under attack, whether from fear, criticism, or uncertainty this week?

Bring those places before the Lord, the One who is your shield. Visualize his protection surrounding you and your loved ones. Let this truth shape your thoughts, words, and actions today, walking with the confidence of one who is fully covered and defended by God's faithful, unyielding presence.

Claiming Your Shield Through Scripture

Prepare Your Psalm

- Open your Bible or write out Psalm 91 on paper. Leave spaces to insert your name and the names of your family members where appropriate.

Personalize the Promises

- As you read each verse, replace general references with your own. For example:
  - "He who dwells in the shelter of the Most High will rest in the shadow of the Almighty." → "Cathy Garland, who dwells in the shelter of the Most High, will rest in the shadow of the Almighty."

Speak It Aloud

- Read the personalized Psalm aloud slowly, letting each declaration sink in. Hear God speaking directly to you and your loved ones.

Visualize God's Shield

- As you recite the verses, picture a radiant shield surrounding you and your family—front, back, sides, above, and below—anchoring each promise in your imagination and heart.

Close in Prayer

- End by thanking God for His protection and presence:
  "Jehovah Magen, my shield, I and my family are covered by your faithful protection. Thank you for surrounding us with your power and peace."

# FREESTYLE JOURNALING PROMPTS

As you consider one of the names from the list, ask the Holy Spirit to show you what this means for your life—not just in the stories of Scripture, but in your actual, everyday moments. How does this aspect of God meet you in your present season? How does this shift how you see yourself, your circumstances, or your future?

_____

_____

_____

_____

_____

_____

Take a moment to respond to God in worship. Using the name or attribute of God you chose, write a short prayer or poem that honors who he is and thanks him for how he is revealing himself in your life today.

_____

_____

_____

_____

# LET'S CONNECT!

I'd love to stay in touch as we grow in revelationship together. Whether you have a story to share, a question to ask, or just want a little encouragement in your inbox, I'm here for it. You can find me on social media or subscribe to the blog for honest reflections, practical faith tools, and resources to help you recognize God revealing himself—right where you are.

## revelationship.net

Looking for more? Visit Revelationship.net for additional resources, including video teachings, free printables, devotional tools, and more to help you recognize God's self-revealing love in your everyday life. Whether you're exploring on your own or with a group, there's something there to equip and encourage your journey.